POACHER JUSTICE

POACHER JUSTICE

By

William Wasserman

ISBN: 978-0-578-90769-7

Cover by John Wasserman

ALSO BY WILLIAM WASSERMAN

Poachers, Lies and Alibis

Poacher Hunter

It's a Wild Life

Track of the Poacher

Wildlife Guardian

Game Warden

Poacher Wars

Trapping Secrets

Pennsylvania Wildlife Tails

In Memory of Deputy Bob McConnell
You were always there for me.

Introduction

For more than thirty years, I tracked down outlaw hunters and brought them to justice. From the big city streets of Philadelphia to the rugged mountains of northern Pennsylvania, I pursued them on foot and by vehicle and by boat. Along the way, I investigated thousands of game law violations and arrested many career poachers.

My patrol districts comprised roughly four hundred square miles where I encountered some of the most unpredictable characters under the sun. Some were likable, others were despicable, but they all had one thing in common: a blatant disregard for our natural resource laws and a sense of fair play.

The incidents recounted in this book are real; however, the stories are based on my memories over a period of years and may differ from the memories of others. I admit to taking some creative liberties with events and to re-creating some of the dialog. I have also given the poachers and their associates fictitious names and have altered their physical descriptions. Any resemblance to actual persons, living or dead, is entirely coincidental.

x

I know what you're thinking: 'Did he fire six shots or only five?' Well, to tell you the truth, in all this excitement, I've kinda lost track myself. But being this is a .44 Magnum, the most powerful handgun in the world, and would blow your head clean off, you've got to ask yourself one question: 'Do I feel lucky?' Well, do you, punk?

— Clint Eastwood (Dirty Harry)
Warner Brothers Action Film, 1971

A barbarian is not aware that he is a barbarian.
~Jack Vance

Of Boys and Barbarians

PAUL MARTIN BROUGHT HIS FORD pickup to a turtle-like crawl when he spotted the deer. There were five of them, all does. They were in an open field, less than fifty yards away. Easy targets to be sure. And although doe season wouldn't open for two more days, it didn't bother him a bit. Nor did it trouble Whitey Storm, who was seated next to him. In fact, the two had been road hunting while drinking cans of beer all afternoon, hoping for just such a sight.

It was November 30, 1985. In those days, Pennsylvania had a two-week buck season followed by a three-day doe season. But in order to hunt doe, you were required to possess a separate license, for which a very limited number were drawn through the county treasurer. Since Paul Martin and Whitey Storm didn't have the necessary licenses, they planned to kill two does on the last day of buck season and get them home without being caught.

Paul Martin eased his pickup truck to the roadside, slid the gearshift into neutral and set his brake, his eyes fixed on the grazing deer the whole time. He glanced into the rearview mirror. No cars were coming their way. The road was empty. Not a soul in sight. Perfect. He powered down the passenger window and looked over at his companion. "They're all yours," he said in a low voice. "Make 'em pay."

Whitey Storm put a can to his mouth, tilted his head back and took a long swallow before handing the can to Martin. Martin obediently set it on the dashboard. He knew better than to steal a sip of Storm's brew, especially when he had a gun in his hands. Both men had violent tempers, but his friend was totally unpredictable, and the slightest provocation could turn him into a raging bull. It was just last week that he had watched Storm level three men in a bar fight after one of them bumped his elbow, causing him to spill his drink. The man tried to apologize, but Storm was having none of it. In an instant, he spun around and brought his fist crashing into the man's jaw, dropping him like a sack of bricks. When his two friends attempted to intervene, he flattened both of them as well. The whole thing lasted ten seconds.

Whitey Storm squirmed around in his seat and positioned himself for a good shot, then he shouldered his rifle with the barrel pointed into the field. Even with iron sights, there would be little chance of a miss at such a short range. Pushing his cheek into the stock, he steadied the rifle, took a deep breath, and centered the front bead on a large doe. Then he slowly breathed out through his nose until his lungs were empty and squeezed back on the trigger.

His rifle barked once, its echo cut short as the bullet struck flesh, boring through the whitetail's chest and bursting its heart before exiting between its ribs on the opposite side. The doe collapsed instantly, as if its legs were suddenly cut off at the knees. The four remaining deer bolted into the field; their tails held high as they fled the poacher's gun. Whitey Storm worked the action quickly, chambering another round in a millisecond. Then he fired again, and a second deer fell, its spine severed by the Ruger's deadly missile.

Paul Martin bellowed a drunken victory cry and dropped his transmission into gear while Whitey Storm grabbed his can off the dash. He chugged down the remaining liquid and tossed the empty can out the window as Martin's pickup rumbled into the field. When they reached the first deer, both men jumped out, grabbed the doe by its legs and heaved it into the bed of the pickup with practiced precision. Climbing back inside the cab, they wheeled over to the second doe and retrieved it in the same manner.

Boomer Smith had been on his way to the barber shop down town when he rounded a bend and saw their pickup truck stopped along the berm with a rifle sticking out the window. Realizing the occupants were road hunting, he slowed down to get a license number.

Paul Martin and Whitey Storm were so focused on the deer at the time that they never looked back as Boomer crept up behind them in his Chevy Impala. Then he watched in disgust as the Whitey Storm shot both deer.

Boomer was a lifelong hunter who prided himself in being a true sportsman. He was looking forward to the doe season opening on Monday, and the fact that these poachers had just killed two deer right in front of his eyes riled him to no end.

He watched as their truck barreled into the field to pick them up. They worked fast, each knowing exactly what the other would do. They'd done this before, countless times he figured, and he couldn't help but wonder how many deer they'd killed in the same way over the years. Boomer continued to watch as they jumped back into the truck and turned back toward the road. He knew they saw him. He was parked broadside to their vehicle, completely in the open as they came charging across the field directly at him.

He yanked open his glovebox and rummaged nervously through the assorted junk inside until he found a ballpoint pen and paper. He peeked up, his head just above the dashboard as the truck came barreling toward his car. Thinking they might ram him, he braced himself, preparing for the worst. Then, at the last possible moment, the driver slammed his brakes and skidded to a stop mere inches from his door.

Boomer could see two men inside. Both were younger than him. Thirties perhaps. They were broad shouldered with heavy chests and thick muscular necks, reminding him of the professional wrestlers he watched on TV Saturday nights. They sat glaring at him for what seemed an eternity before the driver backed up just enough to nose around Boomer's car, barely missing his front fender as he steered back onto the highway and shook his fist menacingly at him before speeding off.

With trembling hands, Boomer wrote down the truck's tag number along with a description of the men inside. Then, with his heart hammering in his chest, he dropped his Chevy into gear and started back home to call the Pennsylvania Game Commission.

State Game Warden Chuck Arcovitch was patrolling the northern edge of his district at about the same time that Whitey Storm and Paul Martin were loading the two deer they'd killed into their pickup truck. He was miles away when a call came over his radio alerting him to an entirely different matter.

"Dallas to five-three-five...!" barked the dispatcher. There was a sense of urgency in her voice. Unusual for Diane; she'd been on the job for a long time. Had to be bad news.

Chuck pulled his mic from the dash and put it to his face. "Five-three-five by."

"You have a hunting accident in Springfield Township," she said. "The state police will meet you in the village of Lynn and take you to the site."

"Ten-four," replied Chuck. And he could hear the gloom in his own voice as he responded.

Like most veteran game wardens, he had investigated many hunting accidents over the years and was all too familiar with the human tragedy surrounding these incidents. Fatal accidents were the worst. Fortunately, most of the ones he'd investigated resulted in minor injuries as a result of pellets fired from a shotgun during spring turkey season, although some were more serious, causing partial paralysis or some other lasting disability. But this one would be a first: unlike any of the others he'd investigated, it would prove to have a mildly humorous side.

16

When Chuck neared the village of Lynn, he saw a state trooper's marked sedan parked along the road and nosed in behind it. Chuck recognized the trooper as he exited his vehicle and walked over to the car. He had a good relationship with the state police, having worked with them on several investigations in the past.

"Hey Chuck," said the trooper. "Sorry to drag you over here, being deer season and all, but we got a report of someone who was brought to the hospital with gunshot injuries, and it turned out to be a hunting accident. It's all yours, my friend."

"Know how it happened?" asked Chuck.

"Self-inflicted," said the trooper. "Kid's name is Spike Torkel. Shot himself in the foot. He was brought in by a friend named Rudy Lalley. Apparently, they were hunting together when it happened. They're both in their late teens."

"Any other witnesses?"

"Not that I'm aware of."

Chuck took a pen and notepad from his shirt pocket and jotted down the information. "Where is Lally now?"

"He's home. I told him to stay there until you arrived."

"Appreciate that," said Chuck. "I'll head over there and talk to him about it."

Rudy Lally and Spike Torkel lived in homes that were a short distance from Chuck's house in the village of Brooklyn. He was familiar with both of them. They were good kids who went to the same school as his two daughters. Rudy lived with his mother, a fine lady who was well-liked in the community. He was sure they would cooperate with him when he knocked on the door.

Rudy was visibly nervous when Chuck stepped inside, which was expected considering the circumstances. After some cordial talk with Rudy and his mother, they all sat at the kitchen table and Chuck took out a yellow legal pad and a pen from his briefcase as he questioned Rudy about the incident.

"Were you with Spike when he shot himself?" he began.

"Yes."

"So, you witnessed it."

"Yes."

"Tell me how it happened."

Rudy looked over at his mother. She nodded supportively. "Go ahead, Rudy," she said. "He's just doing his job."

Rudy blew a long sigh and shook his head regrettably. "We were hunting back in the woods when Spike stepped over a log and slipped on some wet leaves," he said. "The gun went off and he shot himself in the foot. It was an accident."

"What was he hunting with?"

"His dad's Remington," said Rudy. "It's a .270. Made a big hole in his foot, too."

Chuck wrote down the information on his legal pad and looked up at Rudy. "Where's the gun?"

"It's in my trunk. Want to see it?"

"Yes, but not now. You can get it for me before I go."

Rudy nodded in agreement.

"How far from the nearest road were you when the accident happened?"

"Oh, we were pretty far in," said Rudy.

"How far?"

He paused in thought for a moment. "About two miles I guess."

There was something about Rudy's mannerism that gave Chuck the feeling he wasn't being truthful. Years of experience along with countless investigations had given Chuck a sixth sense so to speak, and his suspicions about the people he interviewed were usually right.

"Two miles!" remarked Chuck. "Boy, you young guys really like to get off the road. I used to do that when I was young."

Rudy offered a lame smile. "We heard there was a ten-pointer hanging out back there. Thought we might get lucky and jump him."

"Did you ever see him?"

"Nope."

"Next year maybe," offered Chuck.

"Hope so."

Chuck continued with a series of easy questions: Did they see any deer at all? Were other hunters in the area who saw what happened? What were the lighting conditions in the woods—dark and shady or bright and sunny? Was the ground cover rocky and uneven or coated with slippery leaves?

Rudy answered everything casually and without effort, getting more relaxed by the minute as Chuck intentionally threw one softball question after another his way, hoping the more casual atmosphere would get Rudy to say something inconsistent with his previous story. But he'd had plenty of time to think before Chuck arrived, and his recount of the incident remained solid at first. But when Chuck started asking more pointed questions, his story began to unravel.

"When Spike shot himself in the foot, what did you do then?" he asked.

"We took his boot off and I wrapped his foot in a hanky."

"Could Spike walk?"

"No. He couldn't walk at all."

"Then how did he get out of the woods?"

"I carried him."

Chuck leaned back in his chair, laced his fingers together and stared at him critically.

Rudy gazed back at Chuck for a long moment, then dropped his head and studied the back of his hands.

"You carried Spike on your back for two miles?" pressed Chuck. "That's what you're telling me?"

Rudy swallowed hard and nodded a yes.

Chuck couldn't help the sly grin that crossed his face. "Rudy, you're not a big guy. I know you're probably strong, but Spike Torkel is a foot taller than you and must outweigh you by at least twenty-five pounds."

Rudy said nothing.

Chuck reached into his briefcase, pulled out an affidavit form and set it on the table in front of Rudy. "I would like you to write down, in your own words, what you just told me about the accident," he said in a serious tone. "But before you do, I need to caution you that making a false statement to an officer

19

or filing a false affidavit is a violation of the law." He paused for a moment, allowing his words to sink in. Then: "I don't think you're telling me the truth. I've always believed telling the truth is the honorable thing for a man to do. It's always the best thing to do."

Rudy looked over at his mother for guidance. He could see the worry in her face, and he waited for her response.

"Mr. Arcovitch is a fair man," she said. "Tell him the truth, Rudy."

A look of relief washed over Rudy's face at his mother's words, and with that, he began telling Chuck what really happened that day.

As it turned out, he and Spike were road hunting when the accident occurred. Rudy was driving while Spike looked for some deer to shoot. It wasn't long before they spotted a four-point buck grazing in a field close to the road. Spike signaled for Rudy to stop, and as Rudy steered over to the roadside, Spike reached for the rifle he had resting alongside the seat with the barrel pointed to the floor. He was so focused on the deer, he forgot to pay attention to his hands and inadvertently pulled the trigger as he brought the gun forward. The rifle discharged, sending a bullet into his foot before exiting through the floor of the truck.

Spike screamed in pain as blood began to fill his leather boot. Rudy's face turned white with horror at the sight of it. He decked the accelerator, heading for a hospital as fast as he could, the acrid tang of burnt gunpowder so strong he could taste it as he raced ahead. Because both road hunting and transporting a loaded firearm in a vehicle were violations of the Game Law, Rudy confessed to Chuck that he had made up the story, hoping to avoid prosecution.

When Rudy finished talking, Chuck thanked him and his mother for their cooperation and closed his briefcase. "I'll get back to you later," he said, standing from the table. "Buck season has had me running day and night. Doe season opens Monday, so it'll be a week or two before you hear from me."

Rudy's mother stood and accompanied him to the front door. "I'm sorry for my son's behavior," she said.

Chuck nodded, indicating he understood. "Rudy is a good kid," he said. "He was scared, but I'm glad he finally came around."

Spike Torkel was lying in a hospital bed with his foot wrapped in a heavy cotton bandage when Chuck walked into the room. Spike didn't look surprised to see him, so Chuck figured he must have been forewarned by Rudy.

"How are you feeling?" asked Chuck.

Spike offered a faint smile. "Good as can be expected, I guess."

"Rudy told me everything," said Chuck. Then he opened his briefcase, pulled out a Hunting Accident Report form and attached it to a clipboard before handing it to Spike along with a pen. "I just need you to fill in the blanks, and then I'll be on my way."

Spike took the clipboard from Chuck, rested it on the hospital blanket covering his lap, and began writing. When he finished, he handed it back to Chuck, his eyes rimmed with tears. "I can't believe I shot myself," he said sadly. "I'll be on crutches for weeks, maybe months." He looked away and rubbed his eyes with the back of his hand. "I'm on the baseball team at school. I play first base. Guess that's over too."

"Could have been a lot worse," replied Chuck.

Spike nodded wearily. "I'll never road hunt again," he said. "I promise."

Chuck had intended to lecture him about the incident but cut it short. He could see that Spike was in enough misery as it was, so he wished him well and left the room. On the way out of the hospital he spoke with the nurse assigned to Spike's floor. She told him the injury was serious, but they expected him to have full use of his foot once it healed.

As Chuck left the hospital and walked across the macadam parking lot toward his patrol car, distant gunshots echoed off the outlying mountains. A grim reminder that he still had a long day ahead with buck season in full swing.

He slid into his patrol car and started the engine, deep in thought about the incident. No doubt the boys had both learned several valuable lessons from what had happened, perhaps that was punishment enough, after all, they weren't bad kids, just typical teenagers. Then, as he dropped his car into gear and steered toward the highway, a call came over his radio:

"Dallas to five-three-five. We have a poaching incident in progress. Do you copy?"

"Affirmative," answered Chuck. "Location…?"

"Vicinity of Forest City. You have a deputy on scene now."

"Ten-four," replied Chuck. "I'm in route."

Chuck wheeled out of the parking lot, turned onto the state highway, and activated his emergency lightbar, the incandescent red-and-blues telling everyone in his path to move aside as he hit the gas and raced toward his destination.

W hile Chuck was tied up with the hunting accident investigation, Paul Martin and Whitey Storm were transporting the two deer they'd killed to Paul's house (actually it was his mother's house, with whom he lived) where they gutted both carcasses in the back yard. From there, they took them to an unknown location where they would be out of sight until doe season opened on Monday. When they finished with the deer, Paul told Whitey about the bottle of bourbon his mother kept hidden in her kitchen cupboard.

"She don't drink much," he snorted. "How 'bout we avail ourselves to some of her booty and celebrate our good fortune."

Whitey wiped his bloody hands on the lap of his grease-stained jeans and smiled. "Sounds good," he said. "I could use a little something to warm me up right about now."

Paul slapped Whitey on the back and grinned mischievously. "C'mon," he said. "She's probably upstairs napping right now and time's a-wasting."

Both men hustled inside and made a beeline into the kitchen where Paul grabbed a bottle and two glassed from an oak cabinet above the refrigerator. He set them on the kitchen table, pulled the cork stopper from the bottle and poured the golden-brown liquid into each glass, filling them halfway.

"Have a seat," he said to Whitey. "The game doesn't start for another hour. Redskins against the Browns. It's gonna be a doozy!"

Whitey slid back a wooden chair from under the kitchen table and sat. Paul sat across from him and raised his glass in a salute of goodwill. "That was some fine shooting," he remarked. "Especially on the second deer, bringing it down on the run like that."

"Wasn't nothing," Whitey scoffed. "Done it plenty of times." He raised his glass to his mouth and threw back his head, draining the contents in one hearty gulp.

Paul grabbed the bottle and poured him another drink. "How about that bonehead in the Chevy spying on us?" he croaked. "Like *he* never did it before himself! I mean, you gotta be a fool to go wandering around in the woods looking for a deer when you can shoot 'em all day long right from the road!"

Whitey let out a long and raucous belch. "Yup," he croaked. "Gotta be a fool." He tossed down another drink and held out his glass. "Your mom's got good taste."

Paul Martin smiled crookedly, picked up the bottle of bourbon and began to pour.

While the two poachers were hurling down the hootch and gloating over their misdeeds, they had no idea that a deputy game warden was standing in the field where their deer had been killed, waiting for Chuck Arcovitch to arrive. The deputy had been contacted by Boomer Smith, who never did get his haircut, choosing instead to meet with the deputy and explain what he saw.

"I thought they were gonna run right into me!" he told the deputy as they followed a blood trail through the field. It ended suddenly at a pool of red gore where the deer had dropped. The blood still wet and tacky.

"They wanted to intimidate you," said the deputy. "Glad it didn't work." He pulled a digital camera from his coat pocket and took photographs of the bloody grass while Boomer looked nervously back at the road, hoping the poachers wouldn't return.

"I was plenty scared," said Boomer. "But a man's gotta do what's right...even when he's scared sometimes." He pulled a wrinkled piece of paper from his pocket and handed it to the deputy. "I wrote down the license number when they took off. They were in a red Ford F-150. It had white side panels and a black crossover toolbox behind the cab."

The deputy looked surprised. "Are you sure?

"Sure as rain. I'll never forget it."

"I know who owns that truck. I've even been to his house before," said the deputy. "It was a poaching incident that happened last year. Unfortunately, we couldn't make a case. The guy's name is Stanley Martin. Short man with a slim build. Mid-thirties or so."

Boomer shook his head. "Not him. These guys were pretty big. Rough looking, too. Like the pro wrestlers you see on TV."

"Stanley has a brother named Paul," said the deputy. "He's been in trouble with the law before. Big guy. Drinks too much. Might've been him."

Boomer glanced back at the road for a moment, then asked, "Does he have a big handlebar mustache and hair down to his shoulders?"

"That'd be him," said the deputy. "How about the other guy?"

"Big, like his friend, but clean shaven with short hair...like a soldier or a cop or something." He paused, and the deputy watched his body shudder briefly. "That guy was scary, man. There was something about his eyes...the way he looked at me...like one of those big jungle cats when they sneak up on a deer. Made my knees turn to jelly."

"Seen his kind before," the deputy scoffed. "Mostly bluster, nothing more."

Boomer's lips pressed into a flat line and he shook his head vigorously. "Nope. Not this guy. He's a bad man, I tell you. Bad to the bone. If you're going after him, you better watch out."

Paul Martin pulled back the curtain on the kitchen window and peeked outside when he heard someone knocking on the front door. He could see two vehicles parked in the driveway, one was an unmarked pickup truck; a uniformed deputy stood by the tailgate watching the house. The other was a marked Game Commission patrol car. "We got trouble," he grunted. "Game wardens are here."

Whitey Storm started to get up from his chair but lost his balance and plopped back down. The bourbon had taken its toll and his head was spinning. With one hand on the table and the other on the back of the chair for support, he managed to hoist himself up and stagger over to the window where he could see for himself.

"Looks like we got ratted out after all," he grumbled drunkenly. "I told you we should've dragged that guy out of his car and put a whooping on him for spying on us."

Paul nodded in agreement, his eyes locked on the two vehicles in the driveway. Abruptly, he cocked his head toward the ceiling. "Hear that?"

"Hear what?"

"Bed springs creaking in Mom's room. She's getting up!"

Another knock came. Louder this time.

"She's gonna ruin everything if she answers the door," grumbled Whitey. Go tell her to stay put."

Paul shook his head. "No way. She doesn't even know we're here. She can't tell them a thing!"

Both men stayed in the kitchen where they couldn't be seen and listened. They could hear her footfalls as she made her way downstairs into the living room and opened the front door. Every spoken word came back to them clear as a bell:

"I'm Officer Arcovitch with the Pennsylvania Game Commission. Is Paul Martin here?" asked Chuck.

"I don't think so. He went hunting with his friend this morning."

Chuck said, "We have reliable information that your son and another man shot two antlerless deer earlier today. They were using the red Ford pickup that's parked in your driveway."

"Paul has a hunting license; is there a problem with that?"

"Doe season is closed, which means both deer are illegal."

"Oh, no, no, no. My Pauly would never do that."

"We found blood and deer hair in the bed of his pickup," insisted Chuck.

"Both from legal bucks, I'll bet, too," she countered.

"Then you wouldn't mind if we look around?"

"Around where?"

"I'd like to check your basement and look over your property..."

Paul couldn't believe his ears when she allowed Chuck and his deputy to go into the basement and search it. She even signed a Consent to Search form, making the whole thing completely legal before accompanying them downstairs!

"She's getting old," Paul muttered somberly. "Going senile I guess."

Whitey shook his head in disbelief. "We're fried if they start looking out back. They'll find both gut piles for sure. Let's get out of here while they're still in the basement."

"We can't," said Paul. "The warden's car is at the end of the driveway. He has us blocked in."

Whitey Storm clenched his fingers into tight fists. "I'm going down the basement right now," he said. "I'll bust those two wardens up but good."

"No, you won't! My mom is down there. She might get hurt. Let's wait until they go back outside."

A freshly killed buck hung partially skinned from a beam when Chuck and his deputy walked downstairs. Because the deer was not properly tagged as required by law, and could have been killed by Paul and Whitey, they cut it free from the beam and carried it outside intending to hold it for evidence. As they were loading the carcass onto the bed of the deputy's truck, Stanley Martin pulled into the driveway in a gray sedan. Surprised by what he saw, he exited the vehicle and confronted the wardens.

"What are you doing with my deer?"

"It's improperly tagged," said Chuck. "We're taking it."

"You better have a search warrant!"

Chuck told him they had a consent form signed by his mother and explained why they were there, clarifying that the deer was being held until they concluded that it wasn't killed by his brother and Whitey Storm.

"Whoa! Wait a minute!" blurted Stanley. "I don't know what my brother did or where he did it, but *my* deer was killed legally. I'll take you to where I shot it so you can check for yourself. Maybe we'll find my tag while we're there. I lost it dragging the deer out of the woods."

Chuck agreed to escort him to the location but radioed for another deputy so he'd have two men on location in case Paul and Whitey showed up while he was gone. As soon as the second deputy arrived, Chuck and Stanley started down the road in his patrol car, but they didn't get far when Chuck's radio came alive. "We have trouble here!" a deputy cried out. "You gotta come back right away!"

Chuck slammed his brakes, made a quick U-turn, and decked the accelerator. White passing stripes on the two-lane road became a single line as he raced back to the house, his emergency lights flashing intermittent bursts of red and blue alerting other motorists to move aside.

When Chuck arrived, he saw two exceptionally large men staggering around a deputy's car, punching at the windows while shouting obscenities at his men. It was obvious they were heavily intoxicated, and because they weren't able to break the glass or damage the vehicle, both deputies stood back and watched as they punched away with bloodied fists.

Stanley looked at Chuck and shook his head despairingly. "That's who you're looking for," he said. "The one with the long hair is my brother, Paul. The other one is Whitey Storm. Both drunk as usual."

Chuck took a pair of handcuffs off his duty belt intending to arrest both men, but Stanley warned him not to approach them. "I know you're The Man and all that," he said, "but unless you can call in the cavalry, you'd best not approach those two. They're blind drunk and there's no dealing with either of them when they're like this."

Chuck had a very rural district, and he knew it would take an hour before other game wardens could get there, so he used his two-way radio to call for police backup instead. Still, he knew it would be a while before anyone came.

"I'm not going to stand around and wait for backup," he said to Stanley. "Maybe I can reason with them."

Stanly looked him up and down, then squinted critically. "Look, I don't mean no disrespect, but you ain't' exactly the Incredible Hulk. Either one of those guys could break you in two."

Paul Martin was walking around in a frenzy, punching both of the deputy's vehicles, his fists dripping with blood. Whitey stood by and glared at the deputies with his hands on his hips, his menacing posture daring them to come near.

Chuck thought about what Stanley told him. He hated to admit it, but the guy was right. Both men were huge, and they were half his age. The same with his two deputies. It would be crazy to approach them now. Besides, he had an eyewitness: Boomer, who could identify both men as the ones who shot the two antlerless deer. What's more, Chuck had been careful to take hair and blood samples from their truck before searching Martin's house. He had enough evidence to file charges against them, so he thought it best to let Paul Martin either hurt himself or get tired of punching before trying to talk to him.

But standing there and not doing anything while some drunken buffoon pummeled away at two deputy vehicles just wasn't his style. After a minute or two, Chuck had had enough, so he took a deep breath and started walking toward Paul Martin. Halfway there, he put his handcuffs away. They wouldn't fit Martin's giant wrists anyway, and they'd only be in the way if Martin attacked him.

Chuck was in full uniform as he marched toward Paul and Whitey. His deputies moved toward them as well, intending to back up Chuck if things turned bad.

When Chuck was twenty feet away, Paul Martin, who was still punching cars, wheeled around and pointed a finger at him. "What are you doing on my property?" he bellowed. "You better get out of here right now!"

Suddenly, from the corner of his eye, he saw Stanley running toward his house in a panic as his mother leaned against the open doorway. He quickly turned his attention back to Paul Martin. This was no time to be distracted.

It was the proverbial David and Goliath encounter. Paul Martin was a brooding hulk of a man. He stood glaring at Chuck, his lips curled into an ugly scowl, hoping the warden would come closer so he could pound him into the ground.

Whitey took the opportunity to shout words of encouragement to his buddy: "Don't wait for him to come to you! Go get him Paul and rip his face off!"

Paul Martin looked back at Whitey and then wheeled toward Chuck. "I got a present for you, Boy Scout!" he hollered. Shifting his weight to his back foot, he lifted his bloodied fist back to his ear like a pitcher in Major League baseball and swung his arm over his shoulder, hurling a stream of red gore directly at Chuck.

Chuck stood his ground. He was too far away for the blood to reach him, and he could see it was senseless to try and reason with the man.

Paul Martin's eyes narrowed into slits, his face flush with rage. *"I told you to get off my land!"* he bellowed as he strode toward Chuck with clenched fists.

But all heads turned when Stanley Martin came charging back from his house in a blind panic. "Help!" he screamed. "Mom just had a heart attack!"

Paul Martin stopped dead in his tracks, his eyes wide and uncomprehending as his brother ran over to him. "What?" he sputtered drunkenly. "Mom had what?"

"A heart attack!" puffed Stanley. He turned to Chuck, his face lined with dread. "Call for an ambulance," he pleaded. "Mom's phone is dead. Probably didn't pay her bill again."

Chuck used his hand-held radio to call the Game Commission dispatcher for an ambulance. As it happened, a paramedic who lived close by overheard the call on his scanner and rushed to the scene. He arrived in minutes, a medical bag in his hand as he followed Stanley back into the house.

Paul Martin turned toward Chuck. "You gave my mother a heart attack over a lousy deer!" he shouted. "This is all your fault! You and your stupid deputies!"

Whitey Storm started stoking the fire once again, hurling obscenities at Chuck while goading Paul to finish what he started.

Just as things were looking their worst, a family friend named Al Kutz arrived at the scene after hearing the ambulance call on his scanner. Unlike Paul and Whitey, he seemed completely rational and asked if he could try to calm them down before things got out of hand (as if they already weren't). Chuck was armed, as were his deputies, which meant there was always the possibility, and in this case the likelihood considering his adversary's size and strength, that Paul Martin would overpower Chuck. If that were to happen, he might go for Chuck's sidearm and shoot him with his own gun. Hoping for a miracle, Chuck agreed to let Al Kutz talk to Martin.

As Kutz was trying to talk some sense into Paul Martin and calm him down, Chuck remembered his brother Stanley's warning: *They're blind drunk and there's no dealing with either of them when they're like this.*

Al Kutz was getting nowhere with Paul Martin, but just as things were starting to turn sour again, the paramedic exited the house and informed Chuck that Mrs. Martin did not suffer a heart attack but simply had a fainting spell and refused further assistance. Moments later, Mrs. Martin stepped out of the house, her son Stanley holding her by the arm to steady her as she made her way over to them.

"These men are police officers, Pauly!" she cried. "They wear badges and have guns!"

Her drunken son would have none of it and kept pushing her away.

"They'll shoot you, Pauly," she warned. "You better listen to them."

Paul Martin snorted mockingly. "Oh yeah! We can get guns too!" And with that, he and Whitey started toward the house in a hurry.

Knowing there were firearms on a gun rack hanging on a wall in the house, Chuck instructed his deputies to get their shotguns and take cover by their vehicles. Things were spinning out of control fast. Paul and Whitey seemed crazy enough to come out shooting, and if they did, the wardens were prepared for a deadly confrontation.

But once again, things cooled off when Al Kutz ran into the house and pleaded with Paul and Whitey not to come out with guns in their hands.

M inutes later, Paul Martin and Whitey Storm exited the house unarmed. Chuck and his men breathed a sigh of relief. The last thing they wanted was a gunfight over a couple of illegal deer. Still, had the men come out with guns, the wardens would've had no choice but to defend themselves, and the results would have been tragic.

But their bitterness toward the wardens hadn't changed. The poachers started threatening and cursing at them once again, so Chuck ordered his deputies to put their shotguns away and leave the property. It was senseless to risk a physical confrontation with two lunatic drunks. Chuck wanted to avoid any chance of injury to his men or the poachers. It simply wasn't worth it. He knew who they were, and he had enough evidence to file charges against them. Perhaps, after they'd slept off their drunken rage, they'd be more receptive to answering a few questions.

But it was one of those days where everything that could go wrong did go wrong, and when the second deputy tried to start his truck, all he heard was a series of clicks coming from under the hood.

Chuck went over to the truck and opened the hood while the other deputy searched the toolbox in the bed of his truck for jumper cables so he could boost his partner's battery.

While the deputy was rooting through his toolbox, Whitey Storm, a six-foot-three bruiser of a man who was twenty years younger than the deputy, grabbed him from behind, and spun him around like a ragdoll. Whitey grabbed him by the shirt collar with his left hand and cocked his right arm as if preparing to punch him. The deputy could barely breathe and couldn't break the death grip Whitey had on his collar. Paul Martin stood next to him and cheered him on.

"Break his face!" he shouted. "Go ahead, make him pay!"

Chuck ran over to Whitey, hollering at him to let his deputy go. In those days we had no mace or stun guns to reduce a threat. All Chuck had, other than his service revolver, was a five-cell flashlight made of heavy plastic. Whitely was about to pulverize the deputy's face with his fist when Chuck cracked him on the head with his light. *Thwack!*

Whitey let go of the deputy and turned to face Chuck. "You want some of this too?" he grunted. "I'm gonna tear your heart out!"

Whitely took a step toward Chuck just as Paul's mother appeared from out of nowhere and grabbed him by the arm.

"Leave him alone!" she cried. "You're crazy drunk. Stop this right now?"

Whitey pushed her back, knocking her to the ground. Then he started toward Chuck again, his bloodshot eyes frozen with hatred.

Chuck raised his flashlight and rapped him on the head with three quick blows. Whitey stopped cold and stared at Chuck, rubbing his head, and blinking stupidly. Paul Martin saw what happened and came at him next. Chuck saw him coming and stepped back defensively, striking him on the head with three successive blows, just like his partner. Chuck continued to slowly back away as Paul Martin stopped to rub his injured head. When he looked at his hand and saw blood, he came at him again.

The man was determined to get at Chuck, and there was no doubt in the warden's mind that he'd suffer great bodily harm if he allowed it to happen.

"BACK OFF!" He shouted, reaching for his holstered revolver.

Paul Martin froze in his tracks when he saw that Chuck and his deputies were all about to draw their weapons.

Chuck sensed this was only a temporary lull in the violence and he had to make a decision that might have serious repercussions. The state police hadn't arrived, so he had to rule out their immediate help. Chuck wanted to take Paul Martin and Whitey Storm down, put them in handcuffs and haul them off to the county jail. That, he knew, would involve some serious fighting injuries. Trying to restrain them with Paul's mother constantly interfering would be dangerous for her, too.

Paul Martin and Whitey Storm would not go peacefully, of that he was sure, and Chuck had no intermediate weapons to control the situation. The Game Commission had put all game wardens in this precarious position. Just a year before, they had taken their blackjacks away. He had no mace or pepper spray and no police baton. Only token training with the use of a flashlight as a defensive weapon. That left one option if the men attacked him again: his service revolver. And that was an option he wanted to avoid (things have improved significantly since then).

Chuck knew he had no choice but to leave. Tomorrow was another day. The battle was lost, but the war wasn't over. These men would be brought to justice once he had an opportunity to regroup.

The following morning, Chuck met with his regional supervisor to explain what had happened before he heard the story from the news media. As Chuck filled him in on all the details, his supervisor nodded steadily while taking notes on a yellow legal pad. But when Chuck told him he hit two men with his flashlight, his supervisor looked up at him with a frown of concern.

"You did what?"

Chuck didn't know how to respond at first. Wasn't he listening? He and his men had been under a full-blown assault.

"Why didn't you put them in a 'come-along' hold," pressed his supervisor.

Chuck couldn't believe his ears. A 'come-along' hold is a method of pain compliance where the officer uses a wrist lock, arm bar or other technique to overcome unlawful resistance. Chuck knew that any type of hand-applied force on Whitey Storm would have been ineffective. The idea of putting a wristlock on a two-hundred-and-eighty-pound man twenty years younger and hopped up on drugs or booze, was ludicrous. It would have left him wide open for an attack by Paul Martin. It might even have gotten him killed if the other had grabbed his gun and shot him. Chuck wondered if his supervisor had ever watched any of the police training videos where four officers were struggling with some whacked-out perpetrator high on dope or alcohol. And they had intermediate weapons!

"I did what I had to do," said Chuck.

He knew his supervisor was thinking about a lawsuit against the Game Commission. So was Chuck.

The next day, Chuck went to the Pennsylvania State Police barracks and filed charges against Paul Martin and Whitey Storm for aggravated assault, simple assault, and terroristic threats along with a number of Game Law violations. They followed up by serving arrest warrants on both men, knowing everything would be decided at some later date by a judge.

Weeks later, both men hired an attorney and made a plea bargain in front of Judge O'Rourke, eliminating the need for anyone to appear in court. On the bright side, justice was served, and nobody was seriously injured or killed. In Chuck's own words, "Things could have tipped over on the ugly side very easily, but God was with us."

Several weeks later, Chuck was having lunch in a local restaurant when he ran into Judge O'Rourke. They talked about the incident, and Chuck said he was surprised he wasn't sued on some trumped-up charge in retaliation for simply doing his job. The men certainly seemed vengeful enough.

Judge O'Rourke looked at him and smiled wryly. "They wanted to file a suit against you," he said. "I told them I can't stop you, but just remember, boys, you have to appear before *me* on these charges."

Chuck always liked Judge O'Rourke. He liked him even more after that day.

AUTHORS NOTE

I would like to thank my longtime friend, Chuck Arcovitch for allowing me to use episodes from his outstanding book *A Conservation Officer's Portfolio* in *Poacher Justice*.

Quarry mine, blessed am I
In the luck of the chase
Comes the deer to my singing.
   ~Hunting Song (Navaho)

There Are Two Kinds of Luck

ARCHERY DEER SEASON had been open for two weeks when Billy Roberts spotted a small band of deer grazing in a grassy field along the county road leading to his home. He and Earl Walton were on their way back from an unsuccessful day of bow hunting when Billy brought his Ford F-150 to a slow crawl and stopped broadside to the deer.

"Easy shot from here," Billy said.

"They're a hundred yards away!" remarked Earl. "How you gonna hit one with a bow?"

"Who said anything about a bow? We're five minutes from my house. I can be there and back in no time with my rifle."

It was the last day of the Pennsylvania archery season and Billy hadn't killed a deer yet although he'd been bow hunting almost every day for two weeks. He had shots at three different deer on three different days. Two he missed clean, his arrow sailing high over a shoulder each time. The third, a doe, was hit but only wounded, his broadhead boring deep into its rump. He made a lame attempt to locate the deer after it ran off but never found it.

"I'm good with that," said Earl. "How 'bout we split the meat fifty-fifty."

Billy looked at Earl and frowned. "You're riding in *my* truck, and I'm going to *my* house to get *my* rifle so I can shoot a deer, and you expect me to give you half the meat? Is that what I'm hearing?"

Earl shrugged and turned away. He felt like a fool.

"Gotcha!" whooped Billy. Then he slapped his knee and burst into a fit of laughter. "You should have seen the look on your face. It was priceless!"

Earl whipped his head around and glared at Billy. He hated when somebody made fun of him. "It's getting late," he grunted. "If you want to shoot a deer, you better go get your gun."

Billy wiped the smile off his face. Earl was looking at him with wild, hateful eyes. "Hey, it was just a joke," he said defensively. "We'll split the meat fifty-fifty just like you want."

"We better get going then," Earl said. "It'll be dark soon."

Billy nodded and dropped his truck into gear. He glanced over at Earl as he drove toward home. Earl had his arms crossed and stared out the passenger window in silence. There was something about Earl that Billy couldn't put his finger on. He was a quiet guy. Hardly talked at all, and Earl had taken him for an easygoing lightweight at first. Somebody that could be manipulated. But there was a look in his eyes before that made him shiver. Billy didn't like it. He didn't like it one bit.

Earl Walton was twenty-one but looked more like thirty. He was short and thickset with a broad forehead and a neck as wide as his jaw. He had brown hair cut short, deep chestnut eyes, and ears that were permanently deformed and swollen. Earl had been a wrestler in high school and his cauliflower ears were the result of extensive mat time grappling with opponents.

Billy Roberts was the same age as Earl but much taller. He was six-foot-two with the ropey build of a farm boy. He had a generous mop of sandy-brown hair that fell in different directions over his head as if he just got out of bed. His heavy-lidded green eyes were dark and mysterious, adding to his sleepy-looking countenance.

The men formally met a few days ago when Billy came to work at the paper plant. Earl was sitting in the cafeteria on lunch break, eating a ham and cheese sandwich on rye, when Billy walked over to the table and plopped down across from him.

"I know you," said Billy as he opened his lunch pail and pulled out a peanut butter and banana sandwich on toasted wheat bread. "I used to see you around in school. You were the state champion in wrestling, right?"

Earl nodded that he was.

Billy peeled the wrapping off his sandwich and took a bite. He grabbed a thermos from his open pail, twisted off the lid and filled it with milk. "It was basketball for me," he said with a mouthful of food. "I was pretty good at it, too."

Earl nodded and continued eating. He remembered Billy as well. Who wouldn't? Billy Roberts had carried their high school to the state basketball championships every year since he was a freshman. He was charismatic, handsome, and well-liked by other students, especially the girls. Billy always had a throng of classmates surrounding him wherever he went. He was never alone, even when walking down the halls from class to class there would always be one or two others tagging along.

It wasn't that way for Earl. Unlike basketball and other high school athletics, wrestling was not a team sport. It was *mano a mano*. One against one. And to be honest, unless you were the parent of a competing wrestler, pretty boring to watch. Hence, there were no pregame pep rallies to encourage school spirit and support him, no cheerleaders to cheer him on, and no bands playing rousing music to keep the energy high.

But Earl didn't mind at all. He was a loner. He didn't like crowds, and he didn't like being the center of attention as Billy did. He also didn't like the way some students made fun of his ears. To him, they were a badge of honor. They identified him as a participant of combat sports, a rough and tumble gladiator of the mat, and he wouldn't have had it any other way.

But to most of his classmates, Earl's pale, lumpy ears were the subject of mockery. Never to his face, however, as the one student who made that mistake had his head driven into a wall locker after pointing at his ears and asking when the stalks were going to start sprouting. Instead, he'd hear muffled snickers of ridicule as students walked by with hands covering their mouths.

The thing that bothered him the most was that they didn't understand, or even try to understand, the dedication and sacrifice it took to be a good wrestler, let alone an undefeated champion. Nor did they understand the level of cardiovascular fitness and strength required.

So, they talked about him behind his back and snickered at him in whispered breaths as they passed. And he hated it. But Earl never understood that it wasn't really about his ears so much as his aloofness. Had he been more social and tried to fit in with the other students, he would have had a much better time of it. But Earl wanted to be left alone, be in his own world, do his own thing. As a result, his classmates looked at him as a kind of pariah, someone to avoid and make fun of.

So, when Billy Roberts, who had been the most popular kid in high school a few years back, sat across from him in the cafeteria at work and started a conversation, Earl eyed him warily.

Billy Roberts wasn't used to being the low man on the totem pole. He'd recently lost his job as service advisor at the local Honda dealer and was hired for minimum wage at the paper plant where he and Earl worked. He was making a lot more money in the service department where he was paid hourly plus a commission. But the big money came from the racket he had going with two mechanics who agreed to charge customers for parts they didn't need. If the heater fan stopped working but only needed a squirt of oil, Billy would sell them a new fan. If a hose was leaking coolant, it would be time for a new radiator. Brake pads with fifty percent wear would always be replaced with new pads, even though they were good for thousands of miles. Most customers were never the wiser. After all, a service advisor is basically a salesman, and the more work Billy could convince his customers that their vehicles needed, the more money he could put into his pockets.

Billy had a sixth sense of which customer he could go to, to make the most money. All he needed to do was what he did best: lay on his mesmerizing, folksy charm, and people automatically believed him. His dreamy-eyed smile captivated most of the women—even the grandmas. And most men fell for his robust handshake and pleasant, *I'm looking out for you* sales pitch. But all good things must come to an end. And it did for Billy Roberts when the manager's mother-in-law paid two thousand dollars for a transmission job she didn't need. Billy had no idea who she was. He saw the out-of-state tags on her Cadillac and figured *ca-ching!* Thinking she was at his mercy, he made his move. Because her last name (in marriage) wasn't the same the manager's, he never connected the two.

So here he was, making less than half the money and doing twice as much work sorting paper products on a never-ending assembly line that seemed a mile long. Life could be so unfair sometimes, he thought.

But on the bright side, archery deer season was open, which meant he could subsidize his pantry with venison to help make up for his economic loss. Unfortunately, Billy wasn't having any luck hunting. The fact that he was a lousy shot with a bow didn't help much either. What he needed was a driver: somebody to push through the woods on foot and chase the deer in his direction. When he saw Earl Walton at the lunch table, he zeroed in on him. He knew Earl was into hunting because he'd stood behind him in a long line last year at the hardware store while waiting to buy a hunting license himself. He also knew that Earl was in excellent physical condition, someone who could beat the bushes all day long and not even break a sweat.

"**I** saw a nice ten-pointer yesterday morning," Billy lied to Earl. "Never took a shot at him."

That got Earl's immediate attention. Who would pass up a trophy buck like that? He put down his sandwich and stared at Billy in surprise. "Why not?"

"I'm a meat hunter," replied Billy. "I want to kill a nice fat doe. They're a lot tastier than some big old buck in the rut."

"Where'd you see him?" asked Earl. Billy could see that he was reeling him in. Easier than he thought, too.

Billy took another bite from his peanut butter and banana sandwich. "Smith farm," he mumbled through his food. "They let me hunt there."

"They don't let anybody hunt there," said Earl. "Why you?"

Billy swallowed hard, then said, "My dad used to work for the Smiths. Planted a lot of corn over the years until he got a full-time job in the city. I have the whole place to myself. Two hundred acres."

"Nice!" exclaimed Earl.

"Yup," said Billy taking another bite of his sandwich. "Lots of deer on the property, too."

Earl nodded and started working on his own sandwich. They only got a half hour for lunch, and the minute hand on the wall clock was edging toward twelve-thirty.

"You a hunter?" asked Billy, knowing he was.

Earl nodded.

"Got a bow?"

Earl nodded again.

"Want to go with me tomorrow?"

Earl was caught off guard for a moment. He never expected Billy to ask him to come along. They hardly knew each other, and it didn't make sense that he'd want to risk someone else getting a shot at a deer that he could have for himself. Earl closed his lunch pail and looked at Billy with questioning eyes. "Why me?" he asked.

"I'll be totally honest: season ends tomorrow, and I'm not having much luck with the bow. I need someone to push the woods for me. I'll take turns with you, too—but I got first dibs on the treestand. After I shoot a deer, it'll be your turn."

Earl thought about the offer for a moment. "Fair enough," he said.

"Come to the plant tomorrow morning at six," replied Billy. "I'll meet you in the parking lot out front."

As the two men drove toward Billy's house to get his deer rifle, Earl sat brooding over the fact that they hadn't seen a deer all day until the ones they spotted a few minutes ago. And what happened to that trophy ten-pointer Billy told him about? Earl was in good shape, but he was physically drained from all the walking he'd done trying to push deer toward Billy's treestand. Billy never told him it was all uphill, and Earl was starting to think there were a lot of things Billy didn't tell him.

The setting sun flickered through the trees sending bursts of orange across Earl's face as Billy rounded a bend in the road. "Be at my place in a minute," Billy told him. "Wait for me in the truck while I run inside."

Earl shot out his arm and looked at his wristwatch. "It'll be dark soon," he said. "We got time as long as you're quick about it."

"I will. My rifle is in the kitchen, leaning against a wall so I can shoot right from the kitchen window whenever I see any animals."

Earl nodded thoughtfully as Billy steered into a long driveway leading back to a two-story brick house and parked. "I can taste those venison steaks already," Billy said. With that, he jumped out of his truck and ran across the lawn to the front door and disappeared into the house.

Billy's Ford pickup crawled along the treelined gravel road at a turtle's pace as it approached a narrow opening where they'd seen the deer before. As luck would have it, the herd was still there, ten whitetails grazing peacefully a hundred yards away. Billy stopped broadside to them and slowly powered down his window. Earl had Billy's Winchester XTR Featherweight .30-06 tucked between his legs. He grabbed the rifle with one hand on the forearm and the other on the stock and passed it over to Billy barrel first. Billy leaned back as the muzzle slid past his face and took the rifle from him. Appearing as silhouettes below a darkening sky, the deer paid the poachers no mind, having grown accustomed to occasional traffic on the lonely country road.

Billy shouldered his rifle and peered through the Tasco 4X32 scope. Bringing the deer into focus, he centered the crosshairs behind the right shoulder of a large doe as it grazed peacefully in the field.

As if sensing its impending doom, the doe suddenly looked up and gazed toward Billy's truck. And there it stood, a perfect target, begging to be taken down.

Billy took a deep breath and slowly exhaled. Then he squeezed the trigger.

Kaboom!

The blast shattered the tranquil evening, then fell short as its deadly missile struck the deer and bored through its chest.

The deer dropped like a bag of Sakrete and lay dead while its mates bolted toward a distant tree line. Billy handed his rifle back to Earl and watched them go; their tails held high as they bounded across the dusky field. But one held back as the others raced ahead. Soon it slowed to a stagger, then fell sideways into the grass where it lay dying.

"Two with one shot!" exclaimed Earl. "What luck! Now we each get one!"

"Let's go get them before somebody sees us," cautioned Billy. And with that thought in mind, the men jumped out of Billy's truck and raced into the field.

Both deer were dead when they reached them. "I got the big one," puffed Billy as he dropped to his knees and began to cut into the deer's abdomen with a large hunting knife.

Earl ran past him and knelt by the second deer. He pulled a razor-sharp Buck folding knife from his belt sheath and quickly opened up the carcass, being careful not to pierce the stomach. Reaching up into the chest cavity, he sliced through

43

the surrounding membrane and grabbed the esophagus. After cutting it loose from the throat, he held it tightly in his grip, pulled the entrails from the carcass in one continuous blob and laid the steaming pile in the grass.

Billy was still working on his deer when Earl looked up and wiped his bloody hands on his jeans. "C'mon, Billy," he hollered, "we gotta get out of here!"

"Almost done," Billy replied. "Couple more minutes."

Earl shook his head with a sigh. What more could you expect from a guy who ate peanut butter and banana sandwiches with milk for lunch?

Casey Grant was walking toward his Honda Civic with his bow when he heard the shot. He'd been hunting just up the road, his vehicle parked in a vacant driveway leading to a rundown farmhouse with a FOR RENT sign posted on the weedy front lawn. Billy had paid the car no mind on his way home for his gun earlier. Probably someone inspecting the place, he'd thought. It was the only house on the road for miles besides his own house, and he'd seen several different families residing there over the years. Just one more prospective renter, he figured.

But Billy figured wrong. The property belonged to Benjamin Turner, and because it was still vacant, he'd given his friend Casey Grant permission to hunt the accompanying twenty acres behind the house.

Casey suspected foul play when he heard the blast from a high-powered rifle, so he hustled over to his car and slid inside. It was illegal to kill a deer with a firearm in bow season, and he was upset that someone might be poaching. It was murky enough for his headlights when he keyed the ignition, so he switched them on as he pulled out of the driveway and turned in the direction of the gunshot.

A half mile down the road, he rounded a bend and spotted a Ford pickup truck parked along the berm. Part of the truck was blocking his lane as he approached. Casey recognized the vehicle instantly: a jacked-up two-tone blue and tan F-150 with chrome rails and amber running lights. He'd seen it parked at the paper plant where he was a supervisor on the floor. It belonged to a new guy...what was his name? Billy something...Robinson, Robbins? Something like that. He'd look into it in the morning, he thought as he cruised past the truck. Casey couldn't see anything in the field. It was too dark. He suspected the truck's owner might have taken a shot at a deer, but he couldn't be sure. Distant gunshots have a way of fooling you sometimes and can be difficult to pinpoint. He also thought the truck might belong to a luckless bow hunter who was still up in his treestand. Tomorrow he would come back and check the field, and if he found anything suspicious, report it to the game warden.

Billy heard Casey Grant's car coming long before Earl did, even though the men stood side by side after Earl had dragged his deer next to Billy's.

"*Car!*" shouted Billy.

Earl stood and looked through the trees lining the road. He saw headlights sweep the darkened field as the vehicle rounded a bend, but he couldn't hear the hum of its engine or its tires crunching gravel like Billy could. Earl suffered from hearing loss. The thrashing his ears had taken over the years did more than misshape them.

"Get down!" shouted Billy.

Earl flattened himself in the starlit field. Billy did the same. Both men lay shoulder to shoulder and watched through swaying stems of grass as the vehicle continued down the road toward Billy's truck. It came slowly, deliberately, as if searching for something—them, perhaps, thought Billy. He hoped he was wrong, that the driver was just being cautious, watching for deer that might run onto the road in front of him. Under the blackened sky, there was no way to tell who was driving or what the make or model was, only that it was a mid-sized car and didn't belong to a local resident. Everyone he knew drove pickup trucks.

When the vehicle kept driving and passed out of sight, both men stood and breathed a sigh of relief. "We gotta get out of here," hissed Earl. "He might've heard the shot and came looking. He saw your truck. First thing he'll do is call the game warden when he gets home."

"I'm almost done," breathed Billy. His voice was weak and breaking. "I forgot my rubber gloves and I'm trying not to get blood all over me."

Earl nudged Billy aside and knelt by his deer. "Rubber gloves!" he said with a bitter chuckle. "You can't be serious."

Billy watched Earl ram his arm up into the deer's chest all the way to his elbow. Then, with one quick pull, he ripped the entrails out of the carcass and dropped them on the ground. "Don't be afraid of a little blood," he told him. "It washes off."

Earl's eyes were wide and bright in the moonlight. It made him look like a madman, Billy thought.

Casey Grant went to the paper plant early Sunday morning and waved at the guard as he activated the electronic gate and allowed him to drive by. Casey had been working at the plant since graduating high school twenty-five years ago and was one of only a few supervisors who could come and go as they pleased.

He parked his Honda Civic along the curb in front of the main entrance and pulled a keyring off his belt as he approached the building. There were twenty-two keys on the ring, but only one was fake gold. He had it made at Ace Hardware years ago and used it to unlock the steel-rimmed double doors at the front of the plant and let himself in. Casey walked down a glossy cinder-block hallway that led to his office and stopped at the door to unlock it with a second custom-made key coated in fake silver. Stepping inside, he switched on a fluorescent overhead light and walked over to a five-drawer metal desk and chair in the center of the tiny room.

His boss had surprised him with it last week while Casey was at lunch. A gift for his twenty-five years of dedicated service. He loved it. And why not? His old desk and chair had been there since before he started with the company and had seen better days. The new one was made of sixteen-gauge steel with a high-pressure laminate top and assorted drawers that could accommodate both letter and legal files. Casey slid back the steel-framed manager's chair that came with the desk and sat on the vinyl-covered seat. He loved the chair even more than the desk. It was a roller with an adjustable-height design and had tilt lock and tension controls that let him customize the seat to his personal comfort level.

Casey kept his employee roster in a drawer on his left. He reached down, pulled it open and took out a manilla file folder. Opening the folder on his desk, he paged through an assortment of documents until he came to the roster of employees for his assigned area. There were three hundred and seven names listed alphabetically. He went to the "Rs" and ran his index finger down the list: Randall, Read, Richards, Robbins, *Roberts*...yes, that was it, Billy Roberts, the new guy on the assembly line. Casey reached for a ballpoint pen and pad he kept by the phone, and after jotting down Billy Roberts' home address, he tore the sheet free from the pad and stuffed it in his shirt pocket. Casey looked up at the wall clock. It was eight-thirty-two. If he hurried, he could still make church by ten.

Crows lifted in the distance as Casey approached on foot. There were two groups of them, about fifty yards apart, their broad wings flapping in a distinctive rowing motion, wingtip feathers spread like fingers as they soared toward a neighboring woodlot. The fact that crows had gathered in the field only reinforced his suspicion that a deer had been killed there last night.

Casey always admired crows. To him, their raucous caws were the true call of the wild. His respect for crows began when he was a boy of twelve and had a steel foothold trap baited with fish that was set for raccoons along the Neshaminy Creek. He knew something was amiss long before he got to the trap, for he heard dozens of crows cawing in alarm from a quarter mile away. His pace quickened, and he soon saw hundreds of them perched in the naked branches of distant oaks and maples, their black bodies lined up like soldiers ready for battle.

When he reached his trap, he discovered it had accidentally caught a large crow by a single toe. In the trees above, the others cawed frantically, scolding him to keep away from their comrade in arms.

The captured crow stared up at him with shiny black eyes, showing no fear. Casey marveled at how the crows stuck together. Other birds would have flown off as soon as he approached, but the crows held their ground. The trap had a panhandle spring, and when he placed his foot on it to open the jaws, the crow pecked away at his ankle like a jackhammer. Casey admired its bravery.

When the trap's steel jaws fell open, the tenacious crow hopped free, and Casey watched it fly into the trees with the others. Rejoined by their mate, they began to calm down, the cawing taking on a more subtle tone. Casey pulled the trap rather than reset it, not wanting to risk catching another crow, and continued downstream to check the rest of his traps. Although thirty years had passed, he never forgot that day, and had a profound respect for crows ever since.

He had parked his Honda in the same spot as Billy Robert's Ford pickup had been the night before, and he'd suspected poaching activity as soon as he climbed out of his car. There were two long swaths of flattened grass trailing out of the field to the road: drag trails, he knew, from two deer that had been killed.

Casey stopped when he reached the first gut pile. The heart and liver had been picked apart by the crows, with the only a few bloody scraps left behind, but the entrails remained untouched. He pulled a Polaroid instant camera from his coat pocket and snapped several close-ups. Then he walked over to the second gut pile and photographed it as well.

Casey was puzzled as he walked back through the field to his car. Two deer had been killed, but he'd only heard one shot. It didn't make sense. He shrugged and checked his Timex watch. There was just enough time to go home and change into his dress clothes for church. He'd call the game warden before leaving the house and tell him what he knew. Hopefully, the warden would sort everything out. And if it turned out that Billy Roberts was arrested for poaching deer, his days at the paper plant would be numbered. Casey had no time for poachers. No time at all.

Sunday is the one day of the week that I try to reserve for church and family. But I realized early on in my career that hunting season often meant working seven days straight through from September until mid-December. So, when Casey Grant called about suspected poaching on a Sunday morning, I took it in stride.

"Is this the game warden?" he asked with a gravelly voice.

"Yes," I answered. There was a TV on in the background. It sounded like Fox News.

"Wasserman, right?"

"Yes. How can I help you?"

"I've heard about you," he said. "Tough but fair they tell me. That's the kind of man I like."

"I try," I said.

"I don't have much time. I'm on my way to church, but I wanted to report that I heard a rifle shot around dusk yesterday and found two gut piles this morning. I think I know who did it, too."

"Did you see someone?"

"No, but when I heard the shot, I went looking and found a truck parked along the field. It belongs to Billy Roberts. He's in his early twenties. Works for me at the plant. I found the gut piles out in the field where his truck was parked. They're fresh, too."

"Where did this happen?"

"Warrington Township. Not far from my house. If you can come by around one o'clock or so, I'll take you right to the spot."

"Tell me where you live," I said. "I'll be there."

Casey Grant was a tall, serious-looking, square-jawed man with a buzz cut and unsmiling gray eyes. He wore a neatly pressed Carhartt plaid shirt and dark blue denim jeans as he waited for me on the front porch of a modest single-story house. Casey offered me his hand when I stepped out of my patrol car and walked up to him in full uniform.

"Pleased to meet you, warden," he said.

We shook. "Thanks for your interest in this."

"Not at all," he said. "We have too many poachers around here, anyway." He paused for a moment, then said: "Didn't mean to imply that it's your fault or anything."

"Didn't take it that way."

"Good to hear," he said. He reached into his shirt pocket and pulled out four photographs. "Gut piles," he said, handing them to me. "Fresh, too. I found them in a field this morning."

I thumbed through each photo. "Mind if I keep them?"

"They're yours," he said. "I got no use for them." With that, he turned and started toward his driveway. "Follow me," he offered with a wave. "I'll take you over there right now."

I tailed Casey Grant in my patrol car as he turned down a lonely tree-lined road in his black Honda Civic. He pulled over and parked by an opening that exposed a large grassy field and I pulled in behind him and parked.

Casey climbed out of his Honda and gazed into a flat meadow that stretched to a bank of hardwoods as I walked over and stood beside him. "The crows haven't finished yet," he said. "That's where the gut piles are. The two drag trails you see lead right to them."

Two small flocks of crows had settled in the field a distance away. The more dominant birds picked at the entrails while the others stood back and watched.

"Scavengers," I said with a tone of resentment.

"More like opportunists," offered Casey. "Unlike vultures that only eat carrion, crows eat just about everything; they even hunt and kill small birds and mammals."

"True enough, I said."

I scoured the weedy roadside hoping to find a spent casing from the poacher's gun but came up empty-handed, so I motioned for Casey to come along and we followed the drag trails through the grass, stopping at the first gut pile. Two drag trails told me there were probably two people involved, the alternative being that after dragging the first deer to his truck, a lone poacher doubled back and dragged the second deer over as well. That didn't seem likely. Years on the job had proven that poachers usually traveled in pairs, and I was fairly sure two suspects were involved.

The crows abandoned their lunch and flew into the distant trees long before we approached. Both the heart and liver had been entirely consumed at the first gut pile. The intestines were untouched, as expected, but the stomach had been pecked open. It was packed full of undigested grass, but there were dozens of yellow corn kernels mixed in as well.

Casey stood behind me as I knelt by the entrails and took a pair of blue medical exam gloves from my jacket pocket and snapped them on. After a careful probe of the viscera, with nothing to show for it, we went over to the second gut pile and I examined it as well. The heart and liver were gone, with only a few scraps remaining, but the stomach was still intact, and I discovered a .30 caliber slug lying in the gore-soaked grass when I moved the stomach aside. Although mushroomed from the impact of flesh and bone, it was in good condition and suitable for a forensic ballistic examination.

Ballistics experts can identify a weapon by the markings left behind on a bullet or bullet casing after firing. Hoping to match the slug with the poacher's gun, I dropped it into my coat pocket and began to suspect that both deer had been killed with the same bullet. It would certainly explain why Casey only heard one shot.

"I'm going to head over to Billy Roberts' place," I said to Casey. "See what he has to say about this."

"Want me to come along?"

"No. Just guide me to his house and keep driving."

We started back to our vehicles and hadn't gone more than a few yards when I felt something solid push up against the sole of my boot. Glancing down, I saw a seven-inch folding knife lying in the grass. It was open, the blade and handle encrusted with deer hair and dried blood.

"Look at this!" I said, picking it up.

Casey's cold gray eyes grew wide. "That's a Buck Ranger," he remarked. "An old one, too. Looks like it's in good condition."

Through the thick coating of blood, I could see an inscription on the blade. I rubbed it clean with my thumb and saw the initials E. W. had been engraved into the steel.

I looked over at Casey. "If Billy Roberts killed both deer, it sure looks like somebody was with him."

Casey stuck his arm out the window of his Honda Civic and pointed to Billy's house as he drove on by. We hadn't had rain for a month, and I struggled to see in front of me as his tires threw up a cloud of dust that resembled a thick brown fog. After following in his smoky wake for several miles, I was glad to finally turn off the narrow country road onto the Roberts property. Billy's truck was parked by the house, so I continued down the long driveway and parked behind it.

A modest brick home with two floors and several acres of cleared land surrounded by a large tract of hardwoods, I doubted Billy was the owner. Behind the house, a twenty-foot clothesline was decorated with colorful plaid shirts and denim jeans drying in the cold October breeze.

I went to the front door and rapped on it with my knuckles. I could hear the scrape of a chair being pushed back and footsteps approaching. When the door opened, a man in his early twenties stood gawking at me in total surprise.

"Billy Roberts?" I asked.

He looked over his shoulder into the house and quickly stepped outside and closed the door behind him. "Yeah," he said, eyeing me cautiously. "Is there something wrong?"

"I'm here about the deer you killed yesterday."

"Deer?" he said in mock surprise. "I was bow hunting yesterday, but I didn't kill any deer."

"I have a witness who saw your truck parked by a field early last night where two deer were shot with a rifle."

"Where was this?"

"Township Road 421."

Billy thought for moment, then: "Ohhhh yeah!" he replied as if he'd just remembered something that would explain everything. "That was me all right. On my way home I had to pee real bad, so I pulled over and watered some bushes along the road. That's why my truck was there."

"And you didn't see anyone or hear any shots?"

"Nope. Didn't hear a thing."

"I don't think that's possible, Billy. My witness drove right by your truck, and you're telling me you didn't see him?

"I don't know what else to say except that I didn't see or hear anything."

"Do you own any rifles?"

"One. Why?"

"What kind?"

"A Winchester 30-06."

I reached into my coat pocket and retrieved the bullet I recovered from the second gut pile. "I found this under some entrails in the field. I think it came from your rifle."

Billy began to sense the gravity of his situation and his eyes darted about as if looking for a place to hide.

"I think you should leave," he said nervously. "You got no right to be here. This is private property."

I knew it would be next to impossible to get a search warrant on Sunday, and if I left the premises, the first thing Billy would do is hide his rifle and get rid of any illegal venison he had on the property. I also understood that Billy didn't know that, so I went for the bluff.

"I can have a deputy here in ten minutes to stand guard while I go into town and get a search warrant," I said.

Billy started breathing hard and his face turned pale. "I'm going back inside," he huffed, "and you can't stop me."

That wasn't the response I'd hoped for, but Billy was almost paralyzed with fear, and his immediate reaction was to cut and run.

As Billy turned to reach for the door, it suddenly swung open. Standing in the entry was a solidly built woman in her late forties. She was dressed in faded blue jeans and a gray Carhartt sweatshirt with a zippered front. When she saw my uniform, she froze with concern. "Is there a problem, officer?"

"State game warden," I said. "I'm investigating a poaching incident. I think Billy was involved."

"This is my house. Billy is my son; he lives here with me. What makes you think he was involved?"

"We had two illegal deer killed early last night. I have a witness who saw Billy's truck parked by the field where they were killed."

Mrs. Roberts closed her eyes for a moment and slowly shook her head. "I work the three-to-eleven shift at the hospital," she said. "When I came home, my kitchen counter was a disaster with blood and whatnot from a deer that had been cut up. I saw the meat in my freezer. It's all wrapped in paper. Every piece is labeled." She turned to Billy. "Please don't tell me those deer were killed illegally."

Billy looked down at his shoes and said nothing.

"Your silence tells me all I need to know," she said to him. She turned to me. "You're welcome to come inside and take the meat, officer. I don't want any part of it."

"I'll need you to sign a Consent to Search Form first. Are you willing to do that?"

"Of course," she replied.

I turned to Billy. "I want to take a look inside your truck first."

"Go ahead," he muttered. "You got me cold anyway."

I had Billy accompany me as I inspected his vehicle. There were fresh blood stains, deer hairs, and droppings in the bed, so I grabbed a camera from my patrol car and took some evidence photos. Next, I looked through the passenger window and spotted a spent .30-06 cartridge lying on the floor in plain view, so I opened the door, pocketed the shell, and climbed inside the cab for a better look. After searching for another cartridge and finding nothing, I climbed back out and faced Billy.

"How many shots did you fire at the deer?"

"Just one. Killed them both. It was a lucky shot."

"There are two kinds of luck, you know."

Billy looked confused. "Huh?"

"You're looking at a thousand-dollar fine. It would have been half that if you only killed one deer."

Billy's face went blank. "But I don't have that kind of money."

"You should've thought about that ahead of time," I said. "You can ask the judge to put you on time payments. He usually complies."

Billy looked back at his house. "My mom is gonna kill me."

"Speaking of your mom," I said, "it's time to gather up all that venison. I'll be taking your rifle, too."

"My rifle!" he said painfully. "Man, do you have to?"

"I'll need it for a ballistics examination. I could take your truck, too," I added. "It's loaded with evidence."

Billy looked like he was about to faint. "Are you serious?"

"Dead serious," I said. "If I catch you doing this again, you can kiss your truck goodbye. Now let's get back to your house so I can finish up."

Casey Grant was almost home when he realized who the initials on the knife belonged to. He remembered seeing Earl Walters and Billy Roberts sitting together on their lunch break last Friday as he stepped into the cafeteria and fed quarters into the Coca Cola machine. Normally, he wouldn't have paid any attention to who was sitting with whom, but Earl Walton had worked at the plant for years and always ate his lunch in solitude. The fact that someone was sitting across from Earl, conversing with him, had caused Casey to take a second look.

With the recollection fresh in his mind, Casey made a U-turn and headed for the paper plant. Earl Walters was listed on the employee roster in his office. It would also have his address. Once he found out where Earl lived, he planned to drive back to Billy's place and have me follow him to Earl Walters' house to conclude the investigation.

Casey stepped on the accelerator and sped up. The idea that he could help solve a deer poaching crime excited him immensely. He'd always wanted to be a game warden, but it was more a dream than an actual reality. There had been several opportunities to take the written exam over the years, but he had worked at the paper plant ever since graduating from high school, and in the end, it was simply more comfortable for him to stay right where he was. He often regretted the decision.

After Mrs. Roberts signed a Consent to Search Form, I walked into the kitchen with her and Billy and saw Billy's scoped Winchester rifle leaning in a corner adjacent to a large two-door Frigidaire refrigerator/freezer. I picked up the rifle and opened the action. It was still loaded, so I made it safe and took the rifle out to my patrol car for storage. When I returned to the house, I went back into the kitchen and pulled thirty pounds of deboned venison out of the freezer that had been cut up and individually wrapped in freezer paper. I set the pieces on the kitchen counter and turned to Billy.

"Where's the rest of it?"

Billy shrugged. "That's all I got."

"Two deer would provide a lot more meat than this," I said. "You better start being honest with me, Billy. I can still change my mind about taking your truck."

Billy stared at the meat for a moment, then looked out the kitchen window at his Ford pickup parked in the driveway. "Somebody was with me," he admitted. "He took the second deer home with him."

"Who?"

"I don't know his name. I just met the guy at work a couple days ago."

"I hear the Mystery Man story a lot, Billy. It's never true. Who is he?"

"I don't know his name, honest!"

I reached into my pocket and pulled out the Buck knife I found and showed it to Billy. "This was lying near one of the gut piles. It has the initials E. W. engraved into the blade. I'm asking you for the last time: who was with you?"

Billy dropped his chin and shrugged.

"Billy Roberts!" his mother scolded. "You better start telling the truth *right now!*" Her eyes flashed with anger. "You might be over twenty-one, but you're still living under my roof!"

Billy swallowed hard and I watched his eyes begin to twitch uncontrollably. "This guy scares me," he breathed. "There's something going on in his head, and it ain't pretty. He's got this mean streak that comes out of nowhere. One second he's real quiet and easygoing; the next second he acts like he wants to tear your head off."

"Tell him the man's name!" his mother demanded.

Billy flinched at her voice. "It's Earl Walters," he said reluctantly. "But don't tell him I told you. I still gotta work with the guy."

"I'll do what I can."

"Better watch your step around him," cautioned Billy. "He's a bad dude. I watched him rip the guts out of my deer like he was shucking an ear of corn."

"I'll keep that in mind," I said.

Billy didn't know Earl's exact address, but Earl had mentioned he lived on Cemetery Road after Billy picked him up at the plant Saturday morning. Billy also told me that Earl drove a red 1988 Silverado. Cemetery Road was a rural dead-end lane with only a dozen houses along its entire half-mile stretch, so I headed over there hoping to catch him at home.

I spotted Earl's red pickup long before I reached his single-wide, forty-foot trailer that set a short distance off the road. The carcass of an antlerless deer hung upside-down from a maple tree by his driveway. A bold move, considering it had been killed unlawfully, and it gave me a sense about the kind of person I'd be dealing with. Because archery season had recently ended, Earl figured nobody would suspect foul play, and he was right. That is, up until the moment that my marked patrol car pulled into the driveway and parked behind his truck. It was a rural area, and within minutes everyone on Cemetery Road would know that the game warden was at Earl Walters' house.

Rather than go to the door, I walked over to the carcass and examined it. Because it was hung from a gambrel by the tendons in its hind legs, I didn't have to look hard to see a perfectly round, dime-sized hole behind the left front shoulder. There was no exit hole, which confirmed that this was the second deer that fell from Billy's gun.

I pulled a camera from my coat pocket and started snapping photos when I heard the creak of a door behind me. Wheeling around, I saw a broad-shouldered and heavily muscled young man standing in the entryway. Although the temperature was in the mid-thirties, he was dressed only in jeans and a sleeveless T-shirt.

"What are you doing over there?" he boomed.

"State Game Commission," I said. "I want to talk to you about your deer."

Earl closed the door behind him and stepped toward me. As he got closer, I noticed his mangled ears, the hallmark of a grappler with many fights under his belt.

"I killed that deer with a bow yesterday," he said after stopping within ten feet of me. "What's the problem?"

"I know the mark of a broadhead," I said. "This deer was killed with a bullet, not an arrow."

Earl folded his arms over a massive chest and grinned slyly. "Billy Roberts sent you here, didn't he?"

I ignored the question. "This is an illegal kill," I told him. "I'm going to cite you for it and confiscate the deer."

"I know the law," he said. "You need a search warrant to come on my property and take my deer."

"Not if it's in plain view."

Earl thought for a moment, and I waited to hear what kind of excuse he'd come up with. Then: "What if I didn't kill it? What if somebody gave it to me?"

"You mean Billy Roberts?"

"Yup. I wasn't even there. He called me last night and said he killed two deer and couldn't use all the meat. He said he'd give me one, so I drove over to his house and picked it up. I didn't know that was against the law. He killed it, not me."

I reached into my pocket and showed him the Buck knife I found. Earl's eyes grew wide.

"Look familiar?" I said.

"Where'd you find that?"

"I found it where you lost it, Earl. In the field by the two gut piles."

I expected Earl to cave when I showed him the knife; instead, he got angry. "Are you calling me a liar?" he said acidly.

"I'm saying I don't believe you, and that I'm going to confiscate your deer and charge you for assisting Billy Roberts with the unlawful kill."

Earl's face twisted into an ugly scowl, his eyes turning hard and menacing. "You ain't touching my deer!" he said, taking a step toward me. I watched his hands ball into tight fists, and I suddenly remembered Billy's words of caution: *This guy scares me. There's something going on in his head, and it ain't pretty.*

Although I was in good physical condition at the time, with a background in martial arts, Earl was half my age and outweighed me by twenty pounds or so. The last thing I wanted was a physical confrontation with the man. But there was no doubt in my mind that Earl wanted to pound me into putty, so I took a step back and rested my palm on the butt of my holstered revolver, hoping the gesture would deter him.

It didn't.

"What? You gonna shoot me now?" he snorted.

Earl's eyes flicked to my revolver and back to me. He did this three times, calculating if he could reach me before I drew my weapon.

He couldn't. But I was afraid he was about to try when I heard the crunch of gravel from an approaching vehicle behind me.

Earl looked over my shoulder, his eyes locking on the unexpected visitor.

I pivoted slightly, keeping Earl in my peripheral vision as I turned. A black Honda Civic. Casey Grant's car. It came to a stop along the road at the end of Earl's driveway.

Earl froze when Casey climbed out of his vehicle. I was caught off guard as well.

Casey stood by his open door, twenty feet away, the mid-day sun highlighting his square face, deep-set eyes, and serious demeanor. "Earl?" he called, his voice of gravel course and purposeful. "Is there some kind of problem here?"

Earl shook his head and backed away from me. "No, sir, Mr. Grant," he said. "Just having a friendly conversation with the warden here."

"Casey nodded sharply. "See you at the plant tomorrow. Come a little early. I want to talk to you and Billy Roberts before your shift starts."

Earl swallowed hard. He was visibly shaken by Casey's sudden appearance. "Yes, sir," he replied.

Casey got back into his Honda Civic and closed the door. Then he sat there, waiting to make sure Earl Walters behaved himself.

Earl said, "Look, warden, I'm sorry for giving you a hard time. You want the deer, take it. I'm going back inside if that's all right with you. It's getting cold out here."

"I think that would be a good idea," I said. "We'll finish up later."

After untying the illegal doe from the tree and securing it on my big game rack with three heavy-duty rubber bungie cords,

I walked over to Casey's car opened the passenger door and sat inside with him.

"How did you know I was here?" I asked.

Casey told me about how he went back to Billy Roberts' place to tell me about Earl. When Billy told him that I had left minutes earlier and was on my way to Earl's house, Casey said he thought I might need help and decided to come right over.

"I'm glad you did," I said. "I think Earl was ready to come at me until he saw your car."

Casey nodded. "Earl has worked for me for many years. He's a loner. Quiet and impassive most days, but I've seen his temper flare toward some of the men on the line when he thought he was being criticized. Usually, it was for no good reason, too. I'd have fired him a long time ago, but he's one of my best workers."

Casey looked over at Earl's house and back to me. "Earl might be a valuable employee, but I have no time for poachers. I'm going to give both men the lecture of their lives tomorrow morning. They'll be put on notice: one more incident like this and they're terminated."

"Appreciate that," I said. "They're going to need their jobs, considering the fines will be over a thousand dollars for each of them."

"How about their hunting licenses?"

"I'll recommend three years revocation. I'm sure it'll be approved in Harrisburg."

"Good! They deserve it."

I nodded in agreement, then said, "I never would have caught them without your help."

Casey smiled for a moment. Then his mood turned pensive. "You know, I always wanted to be a game warden. Wish I would have taken the test years ago. Too late now, though."

"I don't know about that," I said. "I'm looking for a deputy."

"You serious?"

"Absolutely. Part time. Mostly weekends with a few nights mixed in. Interested?"

"Interested is putting it mildly," he said. "I'd be thrilled!"

I opened the passenger door to get out and turned back to Casey. "I know a good café that's close by. Follow me over and I'll buy you a coffee so we can discuss this a little bit more."

Casey beamed at me. "I'd like that," he said. "I'd like that a lot. And the coffee will be my treat."

Alas, regardless of their doom, the little victims play!
No sense have they of ills to come, nor care beyond today.
~Thomas Gray

Kill Shot

NUISANCE BEAR COMPLAINTS are a common occurrence for game wardens who live in bear country. Most folks enjoy having black bears around and will tolerate minor inconveniences like having their garbage cans tipped over or bird feeders raided. Bears are opportunists and will eat just about anything, but they are especially fond of sunflower seeds and suet, making bird feeders a prime target in the spring and summer months.

But bears can also do considerable harm to cornfields, causing thousands of dollars in damages. Beehives are another prime target for black bears. Once they develop a taste for honey and bee broods, they will continue to raid bee yards until the beekeeper erects an electric fence. Bears have also been known to prey on goats, sheep, pigs, and poultry.

In Pennsylvania, state game wardens are tasked with removing nuisance bears when a landowner asks for help. Over the years, I handled dozens of bear complaints by setting a culvert trap baited with donuts where the bears were creating problems. The trap was made from a seven-foot length of steel culvert pipe approximately thirty-six inches in diameter that is commonly used for highway stormwater drainage.

Once I had the bear captured, I used a four-foot metal jab stick affixed with a syringe at the end to inject the bear with a tranquilizing drug. After about fifteen minutes, the bear would be sedated, and I would then remove a small premolar tooth located directly behind the canine (these teeth are used to determine the age of the bear by counting the rings in cross sections of the tooth root using a microscope). Next, I would clamp a metal tag to each ear using a special tool. These tags are numbered so the bear can be identified if it's trapped again at a later date or shot by a hunter.

While the bear was sleeping off the sedative, I would transport the culvert trap to a remote location in my district (Wyoming County, Pennsylvania) and wait until the bear was completely recovered before releasing it back into the wild.

Unfortunately, there were those few who would take matters into their own hands and shoot a bear that they didn't want on their land, often purposely wounding the animal so it would wander off and die away from their property. Others chose to make a kill shot and then call the game warden demanding that the carcass be disposed of. This chapter is about an incident like that back in 1989.

Culvert trap attached to rear of my patrol vehicle.

Bear trap with captured bear inside.

Bear released from culvert trap and starting to wake up.

Rosie Graham shuffled across her linoleum floor and peered out the kitchen window when she heard Max barking. Max was twelve years old and hardly barked at all anymore. She hoped it wasn't another skunk. It had only been two weeks since Max came to the door reeking of skunk musk. Rosie had quite a time trying to clean the smell off of Max's shaggy coat. Max didn't like baths and whimpered ceaselessly as she washed him down with a bucket of soapy water mixed with baking soda and hydrogen peroxide. She'd managed to eliminate most of the smell with the second washing, but she could still detect the faint whiff of skunk whenever Max brushed by her.

But Max wasn't barking at a skunk. Rosie would have preferred that, however, rather than the bear she saw from her kitchen window. Max kept his distance as the bear pawed garbage from the heavy-duty plastic trash container he'd tipped over in her back yard. It wasn't a big bear, a sow of about two hundred pounds or so she guessed.

At first glance, she feared for Max's life, but the bear paid him no mind even though Max stood a mere twenty feet away. Most bears run when a barking dog shows up, but not this one, and that annoyed Rosie to no end. But Max's barks were low and labored woofs these days, not the harsh and explosive cries he'd delivered in his early years; hence, the bear may have sensed that Max was no threat.

As least that's what Rosie figured, and the fact that Max was wagging his tail the whole time made him appear even less of a threat, although Rosie wasn't certain that the bear took that into account.

Upset that the bear was strewing garbage all over the yard, Rosie marched over to her wall phone and stabbed at the buttons with a crooked finger. It rang five times before someone picked up.

"Game Commission," came a voice at the other end.

Rosie could hear the garbled voice of a dispatcher in the background, something about a violation concerning unlawful hunting over bait.

"I'm calling about a bear in my back yard," Rosie said angrily. "It's out there right now, destroying my property, and I've got garbage scattered all over the place!"

"Can I have your name and address?" asked the dispatcher.

"It's Rosie Graham. I live on Lonely Road and I want somebody out here right now."

"The game warden for your area is tied up on a hunting violation," the dispatcher replied. "If you give me your phone number, I'll have him contact you as soon as possible."

"But the bear is here now!" complained Rosie. "Are you telling me there isn't anyone who can come out here?"

"Not right now," answered the dispatcher. "But somebody will get back to you soon. Do you have a garage?"

"Yes."

"It would be advisable to keep your garbage well sealed and inside your garage. That should discourage the bear enough to keep him away until a game warden can get there."

"He'll come back," insisted Rosie. "They always come back. You're just putting me off. I want somebody out here right now or I'm gonna shoot it!"

"If you'll give me your phone number, I'll—"

"Never mind!" interrupted Rosie. "I'll handle it myself."

"Don't shoot the bear," warned the dispatcher. "We can have a trap brought out, but it won't be today."

With that, Rosie slammed the phone into its receiver and marched into her bedroom. And there, in the corner of the room, was her .30-30 Winchester rifle.

As Rosie was about to take matters into her own hands, I was miles away, looking for the home of an informant who had called about a baited treestand. In those days, many of the rural roads in Wyoming County didn't have street signs, making it difficult at times to differentiate between private lanes and actual township roads. This was one of those occasions, I found, after I turned off the state highway onto a dirt road that I thought was the right one.

After driving a short distance, I realized I'd made a mistake and was on a private road, so I turned around and started back toward the state highway. I hadn't gone far when a pickup truck came barreling toward me. Skidding to a stop, it quickly turned broadside, blocking the road in front of me.

I slammed on my brakes and an angry-looking man stormed from the truck. His jaw was set as he marched toward me with eyes of hardened glass.

There was no time to radio for backup, he was moving too fast, and I didn't want him to reach me while I was sitting inside my vehicle; it would be too difficult to defend myself. I shouldered open the door and quickly jumped out, preparing for the worst.

"Stop!" I shouted with my right palm on the butt of my .357 revolver. He was twenty feet away and froze instantly.

"State officer," I warned. "Stay where you are." I was in full uniform with a badge on my chest, driving a marked patrol car. He had to know I was a lawman, but I reminded him just the same.

He stood where he was, a scowl on his face. "When you come on my land," he shouted, "you walk—don't drive!"

Surprised that he'd taken such a hostile attitude, I identified myself again and ordered him to move his truck out of my way.

"I ain't movin' it!" he said angrily. "You can drive around it or have it towed, but I ain't movin' it."

The lane was narrow and hemmed by trees. There was no room to drive around his vehicle even if I wanted to.

"If you want it towed; that's fine with me," I said. I reached inside my patrol car, grabbed the mic off my police radio and put it to my face.

The man's expression instantly softened, his eyes displaying a mix of surprise and confusion. "Whoa! Wait a minute. You don't have to call a tow truck. I'll move it but I want you off my property."

With that, the man launched into a heated tirade about a bitter disagreement he'd had with a game warden fifteen years ago, his face beet red as he lectured me.

I waited until he was done his rant before responding. "But I'm not that officer," I said. "I just transferred here a few months ago and thought this was the road I wanted. I'm a little lost right now."

He paused for a moment as he processed what I just said. "I guess you're right," he grunted. "I got no quarrel with you. I'll get out of your way and you can be on yours."

I started to climb back inside my patrol car, then turned toward him. "Do you get *Game News*?"

"Huh?"

"It's the Game Commission's monthly magazine— *Pennsylvania Game News*."

"Can't say that I do."

I reached into my glove box and pulled out a recent copy along with a business card. "There's a phone number on the card where you can reach me," I said, handing him the magazine and the card. Any time you have a problem concerning the Game Commission give me a call. I'll try to help."

He paused a moment, a bewildered look on his face. Then: "What road are you looking for?"

"Fox Hollow."

He nodded. "I know it. On your way out, turn right on the state highway and go about a mile or so, it'll be the first dirt road on your left."

My informant on Fox Hollow Road told me there was a baited area three hundred feet into the woods directly across from his house where he'd discovered dozens of apples and a large salt block next to a treestand earlier in the week. I thanked him for the information and started into the woods where I soon caught a glimpse of someone in a treestand dressed in orange and holding a bow.

I took an orange ballcap out of my back pocket and put it on, keeping a watchful eye on the subject as I quietly approached. When I got close, the hunter turned and looked down at me. A boy, obviously underaged to be hunting alone.

"State game warden!" I called up to him. "Come down from the tree."

I watched as he descended the metal ladder leading to his stand and took his bow when he reached the ground.

"How old are you?" I asked.

"Thirteen," he said. "My mom is waiting for me in her car."

"You're supposed to have an adult right here along with you," I said, "not waiting in a car someplace."

He looked scared. "Nobody told me that. Am I in trouble?"

I pointed to the salt block. "That's illegal," I said. "And so are all the apples scattered around your treestand. Who put them there?"

"My dad did when he put up the treestand."

I shook my head in disbelief. "How long ago?"

"Last week, I think. This is my first time coming here."

I removed the boy's hunting license from the back of his orange vest and copied down the information on a notepad. After stuffing his license in my coat pocket, I took photographs of the bait and the treestand.

"Let's go find your mother," I said.

Mom's car was parked along Fox Hollow Road a good two hundred yards from my informant's house. She saw us coming long before I reached her vehicle and stood by the back fender shielding the sun from her eyes with a hand as we approached.

"I'm with the Pennsylvania Game Commission," I told her. "Your son was hunting unaccompanied and his treestand is baited. Two pretty serious violations considering his age."

In her mid-thirties, she was thin, almost twig-like, her auburn hair combed back into a ponytail. "How are we supposed to know about that?" she asked. "Nobody told us."

I said, "When I checked your son's hunting license, I found a Hunter Education Card inside. He was certified two weeks ago. Violations like these are always explained during classroom instructions. He also received a digest of hunting regulations along with his license. The rules regarding junior hunting licenses and hunting over bait are covered in there as well."

She crossed her arms over her chest and frowned. "But my son has a learning disability. He probably didn't understand the information when it was passed out."

"Did you tell the instructors about his disability when you signed him up for the class?"

"Of course!"

"In that case, we always read the test questions out loud to children who have trouble reading. Our instructors take extra time with kids that have learning disabilities. I'm sure everything was explained in great detail."

"This is ridiculous!" she huffed. "He's only thirteen. What are you going to do, make him pay a fine? He doesn't have any money."

"You are responsible for any fines, not your son. And yes, there will be fines."

"What kind of fines?"

"Two hundred dollars for hunting over bait and another fifty for hunting unaccompanied."

"That's not fair! Why can't you just let us go with a warning? My husband and I are too busy working to read the hunting digest that you say came with his license. I don't even know if he got one."

"If you feel I'm being unfair, you can request a hearing in front of a district justice when you get your citations."

"Oh, don't worry about that, Officer-Whoever-You-Are. We will definitely see you in court!"

I explained the dangers of allowing a child to hunt alone in a tree stand with a bow and razor-sharp broadhead arrows, but she seemed more concerned about the fines than anything else, so I asked her for her driver's license, and after jotting down the necessary information, I turned and started back toward my patrol car."

"Did you get those other guys hunting with bait, too?" she called out. "Or are you just picking on my son?"

I turned toward her. "What other hunters?"

"They were about two hundred yards west of my son's treestand. They have a kid with them. Why don't you go harass them too? That should really make your day!"

I didn't know if she was sending me on a wild goose chase or not, but I had to find out, so I walked back to her son's treestand and continued into the woods for quite a distance (well over three hundred yards) where I discovered three baited treestands, all occupied by hunters, one a fourteen-year-old boy.

After talking to the men, I escorted them to their hunting camp and discovered more bait: Cabbage, pumpkins, and apples had been placed in abundance, and paths were cut through the thick brush to make it easier to target the deer as they came in for the bait. The entire area was surrounded by tree stands so the hunters could catch the deer in a crossfire. After taking photographs of the bait, I inspected their hunting licenses and issued citations to both men. Because they were cooperative, I let the boy go with a stern warning rather than a fine. The men, one being his uncle, would both receive two-hundred-dollar fines and have their hunting privileges revoked for two years. In addition, the entire camp (sixteen acres) would be posted closed to hunting for the remainder of the season.

Finally finished with them, I walked back to my patrol car, hoping to grab some lunch, when my radio came alive:

"Dallas to five-three-eight?"

I reached for my two-way radio and keyed the mic: "Five-three-eight by."

"We just had a woman shoot a bear in her back yard. She said it was destroying her property. Can you respond?"

"Ten-four," I replied, my stomach gurgling in protestation. "What's the location?"

"Lonely Road, Tunkhannock Township. Caller is Rosie Graham."

"I'm on my way."

Rosie Graham's house was at the edge of a wooded area that included some of the best bear range in Wyoming County. When I pulled into her driveway, I saw the carcass of a medium-sized bear lying in her back yard fifty feet from her house. There was a brown plastic trashcan near the bear that had been tipped over with the contents scattered haphazardly about. A German shepherd mongrel was tied to a nearby tree. He barked lamely as I climbed out of my car.

I walked over to the bear, crouched down, and examined it, finding it had been shot once in the head.

Arrow points to bullet hole right side of bear's head.

"Yoo-hoo!" came a high-pitched cry from behind.

I stood and turned. Standing at the front door of the house was a short, squat woman dressed in jeans and a heavy red plaid flannel shirt.

"I'm Rosie Graham," she called. "Why don't you come inside and talk. I'll explain everything."

"Be a few minutes," I called back.

I took a dozen photographs of the bear along with some closeups of the single bullet entry hole. Then I turned and walked over to the house while Rosie waited patiently by an open doorway.

Rosie Graham invited me into the kitchen where we sat at a wooden breakfast table centered in the room. She was a robust woman with intense blue eyes, a broad face and sandy-colored hair pulled back into a tight bun.

"Coffee?" she asked. I can put a fresh pot on if you'd like."

"No, but thank you," I said.

"I have tea if you'd prefer that."

"Nothing for me."

She sat heavily, then rested her hands on the table and laced her fingers together. "I had no choice, you know. I had to do it."

"Why do you say that?"

"I was scared. Scared to death. Bears are dangerous animals. I called the Game Commission, but they refused to send anyone out."

"Refused?" I questioned. "We always respond to bear complaints."

She shook her head in dispute. "The bear was tearing my trash apart, spreading garbage all over my yard. The man on the phone said he couldn't send anyone out."

"I cover a lot of territory," I said. "It's deer season. I can't always respond right away when someone calls about a nuisance bear."

Rosie offered a cold shrug. "So it becomes my problem, then."

I ignored the remark. "The call from my dispatcher claimed the bear was destroying property," I said. "Is that right?"

"You saw my back yard. What do you think?"

"I don't think a bear eating garbage is reason enough to shoot it."

Rosie scoffed. "I did what I had to do to protect myself and my property. I have that right under the United States Constitution, you know."

I took a pad and pen from my coat pocket and jotted down some notes. Then said, "What did you shoot it with?"

"My Winchester rifle." The corners of her mouth lifted into a smug smile. "I'm a pretty good shot, too, as you can see."

"Once in the head," I said, nodding. "A kill shot. Did you try firing a warning shot to scare it off?"

Rosie looked at me as if I just grew a third eye. "Why would I do that?" she said. "It would only come back, and I'd have the same problem all over again. I went out through my back door so it wouldn't see me. The bear was eating garbage out of my trashcan and I had a clear shot, so I took it."

"How long have you lived here, Mrs. Graham?"

"What's that got to do with anything?"

"It has plenty to do with it," I said. "How long have you lived here?"

"Twenty years."

"Then you must know that the Game Commission routinely traps nuisance bears and relocates them, don't you?"

She shook her head and sighed. "I've called about bears before. By the time a game warden gets here the damage is already done. They set a trap, catch the bear, and two weeks or a month later the bear comes back."

"I've only been assigned to this area for a few months," I said. "You should've given me a chance to relocate the bear. I would have taken it into another county."

She snorted bitterly. "This is my land, and I have the right to protect my property. So don't tell me what you could have done. You weren't here when the bear was harassing my dog and tearing my garbage apart. But I was, and I decided to put an end to it. That was my call and my right."

I stood from the table. "I'll look into this a little more and get back to you," I said. "For now, I'm going to take the bear and be on my way."

"Suit yourself," she said. "But I didn't do anything wrong."

"I'm not so sure," I told her.

After loading the bear onto my big game rack attached to the back of my patrol vehicle (a 1985 Ford Bronco), and securing it with rubber bungie cords, I drove toward the Game Commission Regional Office to store the carcass in our walk-in freezer.

I had planned to stop for lunch on the way, but after my interview with Rosie Graham, I lost my appetite.

I had plenty of time to think as I cruised down the two-lane blacktop state road, the office was thirty minutes away, so I mulled over whether or not to prosecute Rosie Graham for killing a bear in closed season.

Rosie was correct when she said she had the right to protect her property, but the bear wasn't damaging any structures and never went after her dog. She didn't have any livestock on her property, such as goats or pigs to worry about, and she wasn't a beekeeper, so there was no fear of destruction to hives. The only thing the bear wanted was leftover food scraps that were easily available whenever she left her garbage out in the open.

Had she waited for me to set a trap, I most likely would have captured the bear on its next visit. From there, I could have attached the mobile culvert trap to my Bronco and taken the bear fifty miles or more away before releasing it.

At that time of year, bears are gorging themselves on anything they can get in order to gain weight to prepare for hibernation. In fact, studies have indicated they are eating typically in excess of twenty thousand calories a day. High-calorie food found in garbage cans fits the bill perfectly, because it's all about calories per hour. They're going for the highest number of calories that they can get every day until hibernation.

I knew from studies that both dogs and polar bears can smell seals under three feet of snow for greater than one-half mile. I also knew that black bears have a tremendous sense of smell and I felt certain that they could smell garbage for a great distance downwind.

I also knew that Rosie had killed a female black bear, and that the typical range, during the day, for females is three to five miles in diameter. Males, ten to fifteen miles. But in fall their home ranges decrease as they search for food and spend their time in an area of one square mile, so there would have been a good chance that the bear would not have returned to Rosie's property once I relocated it.

Had she taken some preventative measures to keep the bear away until I brought in a trap, there would have been no need to kill it. When people live in bear country, the best way to keep black bears away from houses is to keep them from finding food there in the first place. Game Commission dispatchers are trained to offer advice to people who complain about bears, such as not putting out trash until the morning of collection day, cleaning outdoor grills after every use, and disposing of grill grease by not dumping it out back. Grease is a powerful attractant, and bears will literally fight each other in order to get to it. Food scraps in compost piles will attract bears, too; and trash, bird seed and pet food should always be kept inside a building, garage or secure shed with the door closed. I was sure that Rosie Graham was offered plenty of advice from our dispatchers when she called to complain about the bear.

All things considered, I felt compelled to charge Rosie Graham with the unlawful killing of a black bear, so I filed a citation against her later that day mandating an eight hundred dollar fine plus costs.

Certain she was in her right, Rosie requested a court hearing and hired a high-priced lawyer from the big city named Malcom Storm. He was a tenacious defense attorney with a reputation of having never lost a court case in his life.

District Judge Patricia Robinson was familiar with Rosie's attorney. She warned me to be prepared, saying he was the most outlandish and unorthodox lawyer she had ever encountered. And that was saying a lot for a woman who had presided over hundreds of court cases in the past ten years. He was known for his longwinded rhetoric and bizarre personality in the courtroom, and I wasn't looking forward to dealing with his self-important and overbearing attitude.

Not like I had a choice. This was the man Rosie Graham hired to represent her. And by all accounts, his fees would soar into the thousands before he even stepped into the courtroom.

It was all about principal with Rosie. The bear was on her land and therefore, in her opinion, she could do whatever she thought was right at the time. But that's not the way it works in Pennsylvania, or any other state for that matter. Wildlife belongs to all the people, and just because a deer, bear, turkey, or any other wild creature wanders onto your property it doesn't give you the right to kill it.

The Game Commission was created back in 1895 because many hunters and trappers felt that wildlife was being over hunted (which it was). Unfortunately, it was too late to help some species. But there was still hope for others, such as bear, deer, and wild turkeys, three of the state's most sought-after game species. Their numbers were at extremely low population levels and would need protection in order to survive. To do this, the Game Commission created restrictive hunting laws designed to protect what wildlife was left and help them to recover. The effort was supported by hiring state game wardens to enforce wildlife laws.

 In those days, wildlife was killed indiscriminately and sold in markets to be served in restaurants. Deer were shot over salt blocks, and many game species were shot at night with the aid of lanterns including turkeys and grouse killed while roosting. Ducks, geese, and other waterfowl were killed by the thousands year-round, including the spring breeding season, and bears were shot in their dens while hibernating.

But that was a hundred years ago, when the deer population was down to five hundred animals for the entire state. Since those early days, the Game Commission has managed to restore populations of deer, bear, wild turkeys, ducks, geese and even the magnificent elk. Bobcats and fishers were brought back, and birds that were threatened with extinction such as bald eagles, peregrine falcons, and ospreys are now thriving in the state.

As a state game warden, I was proud of the Commission's past history and honored to be serving the commonwealth as a guardian of our wild birds and animals.

Rosie Graham should have given me a chance to relocate the bear before taking matters into her own hands. And although Malcom Storm would be a formidable opponent in court, I was determined that justice would prevail.

And so it was several weeks later that I sat in Patricia Robinson's courtroom when I heard the creak of a door behind me and turned to see Malcom Storm stroll confidently into the room escorting a female stenographer.

Mid-forties, lean and tall, he wore a white three-button Armani suit and handmade wingtip shoes. His hair was dyed blonde and fell into a conspicuous shoulder-length ponytail. We were here for a trial on a wildlife violation considered a summary offense in Pennsylvania (defendants sustain no criminal record if convicted of summary offenses). I could count on one hand the number of times I saw a lawyer show up with a stenographer for a summary hearing (bear violations in Pennsylvania can now be much more serious felonies today). Stenographers record every spoken word in a trial. Lawyers use them for one reason: to trap you in a misstatement if the case is appealed to a higher court.

Not that Storm expected to lose. In fact, I'm sure he thought he would handle the case with little difficulty. After all, I was just a minor civil servant, a game warden with no degree in the rules of criminal procedure or case law. Still, he wanted to be sure he covered all the bases. Malcom Storm was one of the best attorneys in the state. He rarely made mistakes and he never took risks. And although he thought the odds were slim at best, there was always the chance that he could lose and Rosie Graham would be convicted. If so, the stenographer would have a record of everything my witnesses and I said. It would give him a detailed transcript to rely on if Rosie were found guilty and we met again in a higher court, while I would have to count on my memory alone.

But what Malcom Storm didn't know was that I was well prepared. I had to be because word travels fast in rural America. As long as I presented my case well, wasn't sloppy or disorganized, and the judge saw that I had a logical reason to prosecute the defendant, I'd be fine. The worse thing for any law enforcement officer is to present a weak case in front of a judge. Once you lose your credibility, it's gone forever. And I promised myself that I'd never let that happen. The guardianship of wildlife in Wyoming County was too important to me.

I had dealt with plenty of criminal defense lawyers over the years. Some were decent and ethical professionals; others were no better than high school bullies. Intimidation, bewilderment, and confusion were their weapons. And sometimes that was all it took to get their client off the hook. But as long as you had a solid case, and a justifiable reason to prosecute, you kept your integrity. And in the lawman's universe, that was everything.

You could beat them at their game, but you had to be prepared. Battles are best won through planning and knowledge and strategy. In this way, the battle is over even before the fighting begins. You had to know where your case was weak. You had to prepare by looking at your evidence and your witnesses and your testimony and consider how a defense attorney might attack each one of them. Then you strengthened your weak points in order to bolster your case. When all was said and done, I had the one thing on my side that Malcom Storm could never have: I had the truth. Otherwise, I had no right to be there.

Prior to this day, I had spent weeks preparing for the trial by reviewing the Game Law as well as legal documents in preparation for Malcom Storm's grand entrance into Judge Robinson's courtroom. Did I have a few butterflies flitting around inside my guts? Yeah. After all, Storm had spent years studying law in college. He worked for a big law firm, wrote legal briefs for a living, and knew every trick in the book when it came to winning a case in court. And although I had considerable courtroom experience, it was miniscule at best compared to the day in and day out affiliation with legal procedures that most attorneys cultivate over the years.

So I was a bit surprised when Storm walked over and asked if he could talk to me in private before the hearing commenced. I assumed he wanted to convince me to drop the charges against his client, and I had no intention of doing so, but to be civil, I got up from my seat and accompanied the attorney into an adjacent conference room where we could talk in private.

Malcom Storm closed the door behind us, set his leather briefcase on a wooden table that stood in the center of the room, and pulled out a chair and sat down without looking up at me.

I pulled a chair from the table and sat across from him, waiting for him to speak. Storm opened his briefcase, pulled out a yellow legal pad and set it on the table in front of him. Taking a pen from an inside pocket of his expensive suit, he scrawled two words on the pad and spun it around for me to read. MIRANDA WARNING, it said.

"I want to give you the opportunity to walk away from this," he said. "Save yourself some embarrassment. I hear you've never lost a case in front of the judge. I'm sure you don't want me to break your record."

I have to admit, he had me for a moment. I expected him to play the intimidation game at some point in the trial but didn't think it would happen this soon. I knew that the Miranda Warning stemmed from a United States Supreme Court case dating back to 1966 where the Justices ruled that once an individual is detained by the police, the defendant cannot be questioned about the case until the defendant is made aware of the right to remain silent and the right to be represented by an attorney. But I was certain I hadn't violated the Miranda Rule.

"Walk away?" I said. "Why would I want to do that?"

"Because you overextended your authority when you questioned my client without advising her of the right to remain silent. Not only that, you entered my client's property without a search warrant."

"I don't think so," I said.

"Officer Wasserman, surely you're familiar with the most rudimentary rules of criminal procedure: probable cause, constitutional rights, that sort of thing . . ."

"Very familiar."

"Then surely you must realize that you violated my client's constitutional rights. You entered her property without a search warrant. Then you questioned her without first reading the Miranda Warning. And then you arrested her for shooting a bear that was destroying her property—a clear violation of her constitutional rights. I'm giving you fair warning, once we win this phony case against her, my client is going to sue you for violating her rights under the United States Constitution."

I kept silent, knowing that a learned attorney such as he, had to realize I hadn't done anything wrong. It was a bluff, and I wasn't about to fall for it.

"But we're willing to overlook that glaring fact," he continued, "willing to let you walk away from forthcoming consequences if you withdraw your charges against my client."

This wasn't the first time an attorney tried to intimidate me with a lawsuit. It's a hazard of the job that all law enforcement officers face at one time or another. Still, I didn't like it, so I stood and slid my chair back under the table. The attorney did likewise.

"Let's not keep the judge waiting," I said.

The courtroom wasn't much bigger than the average two-car garage, with the judge's ample wooden desk situated at the far wall as we entered. Storm sat with his client behind a writing table that faced the judge's desk on the left side of the room, while I took my seat at an identical table to the right. Behind me were several rows of folding chairs for any spectators who might be present. Today they were empty save my single witness: the dispatcher who had taken Rosie's call about the bear.

All heads turned when Judge Patricia Robinson walked into the room through a doorway to our left. Storm and I rose from our chairs in mutual respect. Even Malcom Storm, who worked for a major law firm in the next county, knew about her straight-from-the-shoulder reputation.

The judge eased herself into a large, well-upholstered chair and looked over my citation against Rosie Graham as Storm and I took our seats. After reviewing it, she read the charge aloud and asked Rosie how she would plea.

"Not guilty, Your Honor."

Malcom Storm looked over at me and nodded as if to say he agreed wholeheartedly with his client's plea. I knew what was coming next. Storm would do what all good defense attorneys do: put the police officer on trial in place of their client. Thus, everything my witness and I testified to would be scrutinized for some fatal flaw in legal procedure that would force the judge to find his client not guilty. Never mind the facts. The focus would be on whether I had dotted all my i's and crossed all my t's so to speak.

Rosie Graham wouldn't have to utter a single word in order to defend herself (although I often wondered if a judge ever assumes some level of guilt upon defendants choosing to remain silent when faced with criminal charges). In criminal law, all defendants are considered innocent until proven guilty beyond a reasonable doubt. And that put the onus squarely on my shoulders.

Storm knew I had a strong case; consequently, his plan was to attack how I obtained it. The attorney had tipped his hand in the conference room: He would argue that because I hadn't Mirandized his client, anything she said would be inadmissible in court, and declare that the case should be thrown out. But first, he would have to get through the sworn testimony given by my dispatcher and by me, where he would try to tear it apart and have it dismissed on a technicality.

It was my job to see that it didn't happen.

"Is the Commonwealth ready?" asked Judge Robinson glancing my way.

"Yes, Your Honor," I replied. "The Commonwealth calls Game Commission Dispatcher Mary Smith."

I wanted her to testify first because she'd been the first one to speak with Rosie Graham. Rosie had called the Game Commission to her property to retrieve the dead bear on her own free will; hence, there would be no rightful argument from Storm about search warrants or Miranda Rights. Mary got up from her chair, walked over to Judge Robinson's desk, and was sworn in. Then she faced the courtroom and sat in a straight-backed wooden chair to the judge's immediate left.

In an attempt to keep things brief and to the point, I asked Mary what was said between Rosie Graham and herself regarding Graham's complaint about a bear on her property.

Mary testified that a person who identified herself as Rosie Graham called to report that a bear was in her back yard and that if someone didn't come out right away, she was going to shoot it. Mary went on to say that she told her not to shoot the bear and assured Rosie that an officer would come by with a trap to relocate it, but because hunting season was in full swing, it might take a few days before anyone would be available. She said that Rosie became argumentative and insisted that someone should come out immediately. Mary told her that the game warden assigned to her area was tied up with a poaching incident, at which point Rosie ended the conversation by hanging up the phone.

Malcom Storm had an opportunity to question Mary when she was done her testimony. Judge Robinson had warned me about his tactics, and he proved himself by asking Mary if she had ever met the defendant prior to her phone call about the bear. Mary said she had not.

Storm asked, "Then, how do you know you were speaking to Rosie Graham and not someone else?"

Mary paused; her eyes narrowed in confusion. "It was a phone call," she said, finally. "The woman identified herself as Rosie Graham."

"But you can't be certain it was her, can you?"

"I don't understand."

Storm stood from his seat. "Is the person who called you sitting in this courtroom today? Can you point your finger at my client and tell this court that the voice you heard on the phone was my client's?"

Mary waited a moment before speaking. "I...I don't—"

"You don't!" Storm interrupted. "That's exactly my point! You don't know who called you that day, do you? It could have been anybody; isn't that correct Mrs. Smith?"

Mary was clearly bewildered. "I guess so," she said timidly. "I never..."

Storm cut her off once again. "No further questions, Your Honor."

I took the witness stand immediately after Mary Smith and testified about my conversation with Rosie Graham, explaining that I found a dead bear on her property and that she admitted shooting the bear with a .30-30 Winchester rifle as it was rummaging through her garbage. I told the court that the bear was shot in the head and that the carcass was taken to the Game Commission Regional Office where I extracted a .30 caliber bullet from its skull. My testimony was short and to the point. When I finished, Malcom Storm asked me two questions: did I have a search warrant when I entered her property and did I advise his client of her right to remain silent before questioning her. I answered no to both.

Storm said he had no further questions and called Rosie Graham to the witness stand where she was sworn in by Judge Robinson.

Rosie admitted shooting the bear, but claimed she killed it because she feared for her grandchildren (who did not live with her and were not at her house when she shot the bear), and for her dog's life, but not because it was raiding her garbage cans. She also stated that she'd had bear problems in the past and that the Game Commission didn't do anything to help her.

When she finished testifying, I reminded her that she never told the Game Commission dispatcher or me anything about fearing for her grandchildren or for her dog's welfare. She had been perfectly clear in her message to both of us: the bear was killed because it was into her garbage and she wasn't going to wait for a game warden to stop by with a trap.

After everyone had a chance to testify, it came down to a final summation argument by the prosecution and the defense. It would be our last shot at persuading the judge to see things our way, although Storm and I both realized that she had most likely already come to a conclusion.

The defense always addresses the court first in summation argument, and when Judge Robinson called Malcom Storm for his final words, he argued that Article one, Section eight, of the Pennsylvania Constitution, provided that Rosie Graham was free from unreasonable searches and seizures, and that she had an expectation of privacy on her private property. Hence, the attorney maintained that I had no right to enter her land or to remove the bear and examine it in order to prosecute her. Additionally, he argued that I failed to read his client her Miranda Warning, advising her of the right to remain silent; therefore, my testimony and any other evidence should be suppressed, and his client found not guilty.

In return, I stood from my chair and argued that section 901 of the Pennsylvania Game Law stated that any officer whose duty it is to investigate any alleged violations of the Game Law shall have the power and duty to go upon any land, outside of buildings, posted or otherwise, in the performance of his duty. As a result, I did not need a search warrant, especially considering that Rosie Graham had called the Game Commission and asked for a game warden to come to her property for the bear. I also reminded the court, that the Miranda Rule only applies to a defendant that has been arrested or detained by the police, and that Rosie Graham had invited me into her house and voluntarily answered my questions of her own free will. There was no custodial detention at the time.

When I finished, Judge Robinson's eyes focused on Malcom Storm. "Counselor," she said, "I've taken into consideration your argument that Officer Wasserman should have had a search warrant and should have Mirandized your client, and that you think the evidence he recovered should be suppressed. I disagree. Mrs. Graham was not in custodial detention when Officer Wasserman questioned her. She was in her own home and invited the officer inside to discuss what had happened. Secondly, the Pennsylvania Game Law clearly and specifically allows state game wardens to enter private property in the performance of their duty without a search warrant. Therefore, I find your client guilty as charged."

Malcom Storm's jaw tightened at the verdict, then he closed his briefcase and stood from his desk. "Thank you, Your Honor," he said.

I knew it had to be difficult for him to accept the fact that he had lost his case to a civil servant unpracticed in criminal law, and I respected the way he handled himself in the end.

Malcom Storm new I had a solid case against Rosie Graham, and his only hope was to get her off through a legal technicality. It's a common practice used among defense attorneys that has gotten many outlaws off the hook. Fortunately, I was well prepared, and justice was appropriately served.

There was a child went forth every day,
And the first object he looked upon, that object he became.
        ~Walt Whitman

Of Men and Boys

Dawn WAS JUST BREAKING on the last day of doe season as Jim Thorne drove his Ford pickup along a narrow, snow-covered road while his teenaged son, Jason and a friend sat beside him.

They were in Forkston Township, road hunting and hoping to find some deer to shoot. Not one of them had a Wyoming County doe license, but it didn't matter. A license from neighboring Luzerne County would do just fine. After all, Jim Thorne never met a deer yet that could read a map.

Luck was with them that day (but as I said before, there are two kinds of luck) because before long, a doe was spotted in the open woods not far from the road.

Dad eased his truck to the shoulder and stopped. "Go ahead, son," he said. "This one's yours. Be careful not to spook it."

Son, Jason eased open the passenger door and slipped out, never taking his eyes off the deer as he worked a round into the chamber of his bolt action rifle and leaned over the hood of his father's truck. It was an easy shot. Less than fifty yards separated him from the deer. He squinted into his Tasco scope and set the crosshairs just behind the deer's front shoulder. Then, just like his father had told him, he took a breath and slowly exhaled, emptying his lungs before squeezing the trigger. The rifle thundered under a heavy gray sky, recoiling solidly into Jason's shoulder as it discharged its fatal bullet.

Young Jason had made a perfect shot to the heart, dropping the unsuspecting doe like a bag of cement.

"Quick boys," Thorne called as he bailed out of the truck. "Let's get it loaded."

The three poachers charged through the snowfield and admired their kill. Then father and son each grabbed a front leg and began dragging the limp carcass back toward the road.

In a home not far away, an elderly couple named Henry and Mildred sat on a leather couch in their living room in front of a fire watching TV. It was a cold winter morning and the snow had piled up overnight. A good day to stay home and stay warm, thought Henry. He rose from the couch to add another log to the fireplace and glanced out the picture window as a dark green pickup truck cruised slowly down the county road past his house. Henry bent over slowly and grabbed two oak logs, laying them into the fire with care, then he walked back to the couch and sat next to his wife. Only a few minutes passed when he heard a shot ring out.

"Did you hear that?" he asked, turning toward his wife.

Mildred sat in a trance-like stare watching *General Hospital*. She didn't hear the shot and she didn't hear Henry. Mob boss Victor Jerome had just died after escaping from jail, and Lucy Coe took off with his stolen diamonds. She felt sorry for Lucy because Victor Jerome never loved her, even though he told her he did over and over again. It was her favorite soap opera, and she was completely absorbed as the story unfolded.

Henry smiled at her and started toward the back door. They had to be close, he thought, the shot was pretty loud and there was a small herd of deer that had been hanging around for the past two weeks. Henry suspected road hunters were in the truck that passed his house. Thinking he might be able to catch them in the act, he threw on a coat, grabbed his keys, and hustled out the door to his car parked under the protective roof of an open shed.

With no snow to brush off his windows, he was able to start his 1983 Chevy and head down the road in a matter of seconds. Driving in the direction of the shot, he soon spotted the green pickup.

Jim Thorne had just finished loading the carcass and turned briefly when Henry's Chevy crested a hill and came into view. Not wanting to get caught with an illegal deer, he slammed the tailgate shut and jumped into his truck along with the two boys. Thorne glanced into the rearview mirror as he started the engine and pulled onto the county road, driving away in a casual pace as if nothing were wrong.

Had the car been five minutes earlier, they might've seen Jason shooting from the road, thought Thorne. But the deer had been loaded in his truck and they didn't see anything suspicious. Everything was going to be okay. Hunting season was open, and there wasn't a game warden around for miles. All they had to do was drive a short distance until they reached the Luzerne County line and they'd be home free.

I was close to town when I received a radio message from a Game Commission dispatcher advising me to call Henry about a possible road hunting incident, so I stopped at a phone booth and dialed the number he'd given me. Henry picked up right away, explaining what had happened. He went on to tell me that he could see where a deer had been dragged out of the woods through the snow and suspected the deer had been shot from the road. He asked if I could come by for a look.

"I sure can," I told him.

"That's good," said Henry. "There were three of them. Two were just kids…looked like teenagers to me."

"Where did this happen?"

"I live on Sully Road. I'm the only house. It's a log home with a red car shed alongside of it. Go past my place about two hundred yards and you'll see a bloody drag trail coming out of the woods on the right side of the road. Can't miss it with all the snow. Clear as a bell."

90

Henry gave me a description of the truck and the tag number from the back bumper. I thanked him for the information and headed his way.

Sully Road ran in a half-circle, coming off the state highway near Tunkhannock and reconnected a mile down the road. It was remote, and I could see why someone would choose that location to poach deer as I pulled my patrol car off the road and parked by the drag trail that Henry had discovered. After climbing out of my vehicle to inspect the scene, I could clearly see tire tracks from where the poachers had pulled over and stopped to shoot at the deer. There was a bloody swath in the snow where the deer had been dragged out of the woods and loaded into their truck, and a spent casing from a .30 caliber rifle lay in the road next to the tire tracks. I picked it off the ground and pocketed it before following the drag trail back into the woods. It was littered with the footprints of three individuals, and I only went a short distance before finding where the deer had been killed. It hadn't been gutted, and certainly hadn't been tagged; they were in too much of a hurry to do either.

After taking several photographs of the crime scene, I walked back to my patrol vehicle and called the Game Commission dispatcher for information on the vehicle tag number Henry had provided for me. It came back to an address in Luzerne County, so I started my engine and drove toward Jim Thorne's home.

A freshly killed doe hung from a tree by its neck in front of Thorne's single-story brick home on Church Street. It had been gutted and tagged (accomplished along some back road on the way home), giving it the appearance of a legal kill. I parked my vehicle in front of Thorne's house and stepped over to the deer. There was a single bullet hole behind the right shoulder. No exit wound. The tag attached to its ear was from a Luzerne County antlerless license. I untied the rope from around the tree and lowered the carcass to the ground for a closer look. The name and address written on the tag belonged to Jim Thorne's son, Jason.

Although I suspected this was the doe that had been killed in Wyoming County, I couldn't prove it and thought it best not to confiscate the animal before I spoke with Thorne. I photographed the deer for evidence and walked over to the house and knocked on the front door. No one answered, although Thorne's pickup truck was parked in the driveway. I had a hunch that Thorne was watching, so I walked back to the deer carcass, dragged it over to my patrol car and placed it on the big game carrier attached to the rear of my vehicle, hoping my actions would lure him out.

As I was securing the deer to my game carrier, I heard a voice call out from behind: "Hello, officer. Is something wrong?"

I turned to see Jim Thorne standing in his open doorway dressed in jeans and a heavy Woolrich shirt.

I walked over to him and explained that I suspected the deer had been killed in Wyoming County."

Thorne played it cool, keeping a straight face. "Why do you say that?" he asked.

I told him that I had a witness who saw him with two boys as they were pulling away from an area where a doe had been shot from the road this morning, explaining further that the informant had given me a description of his vehicle and the tag number.

Thorne looked over my shoulder at the deer then back to me. "I was afraid of that," he said soberly. Stepping back into the doorway, he motioned me into his house with a sweep of his hand, "Come on, warden," he said. "Let's get this over with."

I stepped inside with him and explained that my informant was willing to testify and that he could positively identify one of the boys who was with him. I described the boy, then asked if it was his son, Jason.

Thorne let out a heavy sigh. "It's not his fault," he said. "I told him to do it. It was all my idea."

"Who was the other boy?"

"I don't know."

"Look," I said. "You can cooperate and tell me the truth, and maybe get a break, or you can play games and pretend you don't know who was in your truck with you. The harder you make it for me, the harder I'll make it for you. Right now, all three of you could be prosecuted for possessing an unlawfully killed deer. It doesn't necessarily have to be that way."

Thorne looked down and shook his head with regret. "All I ask is that you leave the boys out of this. I'll pay all the fines. It's all my fault."

"Who is the other boy?" I asked again.

"He's my son's buddy from school. His name is Bobby Grover. He lives just down the road. Both boys are at Bobby's house right now."

It bothered me more than a little that Thorne was teaching not only his son, but his neighbor's son to be outlaw hunters. "Why are you doing this?" I said.

"Doing what?"

"Teaching these kids to be poachers."

"I wanted them to have a good time. That's all. It's no fun when you hunt all day and don't see anything. Besides, I only see my son on weekends. His grandparents are raising him."

That's probably a good thing, I thought.

"It's just one deer," he continued, "a few miles over the county line. Can't you give us a break?"

I didn't know what to say, and I didn't think my lecturing him about ethical hunting and good sportsmanship would change his mind. My only hope was that a hefty penalty might persuade him to think twice next time.

"I'm not going to prosecute the boys," I said, "but I will be in touch with Jason's grandparents and Bobby Grover's parents. They need to know what happened today."

Thorne's face screwed into a pout. "Do you really think that's necessary?"

"They're both juveniles. I'm obligated to do that. "And I'll be filing charges against you for shooting a deer from the road, failure to properly tag it, and killing it without the proper license—just to name a few off the top of my head."

Thorne looked worried. "How much is the fine?"

"It'll be over a thousand dollars."

He winced at the cost. "Man, that's gonna hurt."

"And there will be the loss of your hunting license for at least a year," I added.

Thorne nodded gloomily. "Understood."

"You'll receive your citations in the mail later this week," I said. "And I'll be taking your deer on my way out."

"Whoa, officer. I'll pay my fine, but can't you let my son keep the deer?"

"Poaching has consequences," I told him. "Hopefully, your son will understand that concept when he sees an empty rope dangling by the tree out front."

"I wish you didn't have to do that," he said. There was urgency in his voice.

"Me too," I told him.

Hunting pressure was heavy as I resumed my patrol that morning, and it wasn't long before I happened across three hunters dressed in full orange safety clothing on their way out of a wooded area bordering the highway. I often stop for a few minutes of friendly conversation with hunters as I cruise through the county. Usually, I'll ask if they've seen many deer and whether they've heard much shooting in the area. I often won't bother to check their licenses, as I merely want to get a feel for what's going on in my district throughout the season. What better way than to converse with those who are out there participating in the hunt?

I pulled into an open area by the road and parked next to a Dodge Power Wagon that I assumed belonged to one of the men. As they approached, I sensed something wasn't quite right with one of them. He seemed nervous and hung back as the other two came forward. He was younger than they were, a teenager, and he wasn't carrying a rifle.

"How was the hunting today," I asked.

The two hunters exchanged glances, then one of them, the taller of the two, spoke: "Didn't see a thing," he said. "Thought we'd try someplace else."

He was in his mid-thirties and wore a full beard and thick, steel-rimmed glasses.

"There's a lot of pressure in the State Game Lands a few miles from here," I said. "That might get the deer moving for you."

The tall man nodded appreciatively. "Thanks. We'll check it out."

I looked at the other. He was overweight and red-faced. His beathing came in labored puffs. "Did you do a lot of walking today?" I asked.

"Yeah," he said. "As you can see, I'm not in the best physical shape. Can't keep up with Albert anymore."

The tall man smiled. "I keep telling you to go on a diet, Frankie."

Frankie sneered at Albert, then looked at me. "Can we be on our way, officer? We only have a couple more hours before I have to be at work."

I looked at the teenager. He stood ten feet back from the other two, pretending to search for passing birds under a heavy gray sky. "What's your name?" I said.

He looked left and right, as if I might have been asking someone else. "Who? Me?"

Frankie said, "That's Michael. My cousin. Just showing him the ropes, hoping to see a deer."

Convinced that something was going on here, I asked to see everyone's hunting license, starting with Albert and then Frankie. After finding nothing out of order, I stepped over to Michael and asked him to turn around.

When he did, I saw two separate doe licenses attached to the back of his vest, both contained in plastic holders. Hunters could only have one to be legal.

"What's this all about?" I asked.

"What's what all about?"

"You have two doe licenses on your back."

"I do?"

I pulled the cardboard licenses out of their holders and looked them over. One belonged to Michael and gave his age as seventeen. The other belonged to a man named Henry. Michael's doe license was missing its tag but the other one had a tag still attached.

"I see you killed a doe," I said. "Your tag is gone."

Michael turned to face me. "That's right. Last week."

"Where is Henry?"

"He's not here."

"I can see that," I said. "Where is he?"

Michael shrugged. "I don't know."

"Why do you have his license?"

"I didn't know it was there," he said. "I grabbed the vest on my way out the door this morning and never looked at it. Besides, I'm not hunting today. I don't even have a gun."

I suspected that Michael had brought the other license with him hoping to kill a deer and get it home as if legally tagged.

I asked, "Did you leave a gun back in the woods when you saw me coming?"

Michael shook his head emphatically. "No," he insisted. "I don't have a gun and I'm not hunting today."

"I'm going to follow your tracks and see for myself. Are you sure you don't have something to tell me?"

"I'm sure."

I only walked out about twenty-five yards when Michael called after me.

"You're right," he said. "I have a rifle hidden in the brush. I'll show you where it is."

I waited for Michael to catch up and followed him a short distance into the woods where I found a rifle leaning against a pine tree. I picked it off the ground and worked the action, ejecting five rounds.

"So, what's the real story with Henry?" I asked. Then answering for him, I said: "It's the last day of doe season and he couldn't get out, so he asked you to kill a deer for him. Does that about sum it up?"

Michael pressed his lips into a thin line and nodded. "Yes, sir."

I was glad he finally admitted the truth, but the fact that his cousin, Frankie, and his friend Albert stood by and allowed this charade to take place bothered me. They knew exactly what was going on. Frankie even tried to cover for Michael by asking if they could be on their way claiming he had to get to work, hoping I would leave before checking their licenses. There wasn't much I could do about it, but the fact that two older men had allowed their younger companion to willfully lie to me, and another man had allowed him to take his doe license and "fill the tag" because he wouldn't have a chance to hunt that day was upsetting. What a wonderful way to teach a seventeen-year-old how to grow up.

"You're looking at a substantial fine," I said to Michael.

"How much?"

"Six hundred dollars."

He looked shocked. "But I don't have that kind of money," he said. "I'm trying to save for college and can't afford to pay that much."

"Have you ever done anything like this before?"

"No, never. I swear! Henry is my cousin, Frankie too. They both told me it would be okay—that it was only one deer and that it didn't matter as long as it had somebody's tag on it."

"Albert and your two cousins could be prosecuted as well," I said. "Henry for lending you his license (extremely difficult to prove, and I had no intention of pursuing it), and the others for encouraging you to hunt without a doe license. If I were you, I'd ask them to cough up a portion of the fine money."

Michael shook his head vigorously. "Henry doesn't have a job. He was fired again. Frankie is too cheap, and Albert isn't much better. They won't help me."

"I might be able to persuade them to change their minds," I said.

Michael cocked his head and eyed me warily. "But how?"

"Follow me," I said.

When Frankie and Albert saw me returning with Michael and his rifle, they both cringed.

Frankie was first to speak: "I tried to tell him not to come with us, officer, but he insisted."

Albert chimed in next: "And I didn't know Michael had two doe licenses on his vest."

"I find that hard to believe," I said. "As far as I'm concerned, you're both looking at sizeable fines."

Frankie and Albert exchanged nervous glances. "How much?" asked Albert.

I shrugged. "Depends."

They looked at each other again, bewildered by my response.

"Depends on what?" asked Franke.

"Depends on whether you two are going to contribute toward Michael's fine or not. He's looking at six hundred dollars and needs a little financial help."

Frankie grew suspicious. "What do we get out of it?"

"It's more like what you don't get." I said.

"Huh?" they replied in unison.

"You both have aided and abetted Michael by allowing him to hunt with Henry's doe license in order to kill a deer unlawfully. You could each be liable for the same fine as Michael." I paused for a moment to let my words sink in. "There are three of you here," I continued, "all involved in the same violation. If you'll all agree to split the six-hundred-dollar fine evenly, I'll be on my way."

Frankie and Albert seemed to be weighing what I said, then: "I think we can do that," said Frankie. "After all, Michael is family."

I stifled a laugh considering how he was about to walk away from him just a minute earlier. "Michael will receive a citation in the mail later this week," I said. "See that our agreement is followed."

I motioned for Michael to follow me and we both walked over to my patrol car. "Think you can stay out of trouble after this?" I asked.

He nodded. "Thanks for doing what you did back there. I never expected it."

"Don't let it happen again," I cautioned as I opened the driver's door. "Next time you're on your own."

"You have my word."

"A man is only as good as his word," I said, sliding into my patrol car. "I want you to remember that."

Michael nodded that he understood as I keyed the ignition and dropped my Bronco into gear. "Go on back with your cousin," I said. Then I nosed my vehicle onto the highway and made my way toward a large tract of State Game Lands in Noxen Township.

I had only traveled a few miles when I started across a bridge high above the Susquehanna River and spotted two young boys playing along a sheet of ice that had formed along its banks. River ice is especially dangerous as it's weaker than lake ice due to constant shifting from the steady current below, which contributes to thinning ice along shelf-like formations.

The ice extended twenty feet from the bank, and one of the boys was standing at the edge, peering into the dark, frigid water. If the shelf broke under his feet, he would plunge into the river and be swept downstream in seconds. The current was far too strong for anyone to swim ashore, and the slippery ice formation would make it impossible to pull himself from harm's way.

Fearing for their lives, I pulled my car to the roadside and stopped, my eyes riveted on the boy standing on the rim of ice peering into the black swirling water as if mesmerized by the current as it surged and rolled mere inches from his feet.

I shouldered open my door and ran to the edge of the bridge. The boys were a good fifty feet below and a hundred yards downstream from me.

"Get off the ice!" I hollered down at them, my voice thick and rasping in the blustery wind.

Both boys looked up. The one along the dangerous edge of ice seemed dazed as he stared at me. I hollered at him again, ordering him to get off the ice. Suddenly he snapped out of his trance and turned on his heels running toward the other boy who was standing safely along the bank. When he reached him, they both got on their bicycles and started riding away from me along the shelf of ice.

Concerned for their safety, I hustled back to my Bronco and headed down to the river. There was a dirt two-track that ran along the river bank, so I followed it until I came to a narrow lane that led down to the river. I spotted the boys coming my way, but when they saw me, they peddled faster, hoping I wouldn't intercept them before they got away. I can't say that I blame them, after all, moments earlier I was standing on a bridge far above hollering at them to get off the ice.

I exited my patrol car and started making my way toward them on foot, but before I reached them, they jumped off their bikes and started running up the bank toward the woods. They were pretty fast, I must admit. But I've chased a few people in my day and soon intercepted them.

As I approached, I put on a friendly face, hoping not to scare them off again. They looked like twins about twelve years old.

"Hey boys, I'm not going to yell at you," I said. "I just want to talk."

"Are you gonna arrest us?" one asked.

"No, but you shouldn't be playing along the ice. It's dangerous."

"We know," said the boy who had been staring down into the water before.

"Do you know what would happen if you fell into the river?"

"You would drown," came his honest reply. The other boy ran his index finger across his neck, as if it were a knife, which told me he was in accordance with his brother's opinion.

Surprised they were aware of the danger, I asked if their parents knew that they were playing on the river ice.

"Oh sure," came their reply. "They said it would be okay as long as we stayed close to the bank."

The wind began to pick up and I pulled my jacket collar over my neck. "But you both weren't along the bank, were you?" I said.

They looked up at me in silence There was no need to reply.

"Look guys," I said. "I grew up running traplines along the river, but I stayed away from thin ice. I'm not trying to ruin your fun or give you a bad time. I just don't want to see you get hurt, so I'm giving you both an official order to stay off the ice. Okay?"

Both boys promised that they would stay away from the ice, so I thanked them and started walking back to my patrol car.

"Hey, mister," one of them called.

I turned to face them. "Yes?"

"How do you get to be a game warden?"

I smiled. "Stay in school, study hard, and you can be anything you want."

Both boys nodded that they understood, and I watched as they hopped on their bikes and peddled toward home.

Tell the boys I've got the Luck with me now.
~Bret Hart
The luck of Roaring Camp

Roaring Camp

SKUNKS ARE MOSTLY INACTIVE in winter, living off the fat stored in their bodies through summer and fall. Pennsylvania state game wardens are tasked with many duties aside from daily law enforcement patrols. For instance, handling nuisance wildlife complaints was a routine part of my job, skunks being last on my list of favorites. And on this particular winter day—the first Saturday of buck season, no less, I got a call on my two-way radio about a skunk that had entered a house in the borough of Tunkhannock.

Fortunately, I was close by. Had the call come a little later in the day, I would have been miles away in a remote section of Forkston Township, which is where I was headed.

I turned my patrol car around and drove directly into town. After all, what could be worse than having a skunk invade your home, especially if it had worked its way inside.

After locating the house, I parked my patrol car and stepped out. The pungent, sulfur-like scent of skunk musk filled the air as I walked to the front door and knocked. Moments later, a frail-looking woman in her fifties answered, worry written on her face.

"Thank you for coming, officer," she said.

"Is the skunk inside your house?" I asked.

She shook her head. "It tried to get inside, but it got stuck in the wall and started spraying all over the place. It's around back, near the garage door."

Curious, I walked to the back yard for a look before bringing any equipment from my vehicle along. To my surprise, when I turned the corner, I saw the hind end of a skunk sticking out of the stone foundation. I had delt with many skunks over the years, but this was the first time that I had only the business end of a striped stinker to deal with.

The skunk had found a narrow opening between two large stones in the exterior wall and decided to investigate, but it didn't realize its body was wider than its head and kept crawling into the crevice until its shoulders were wedged tightly between the stones (*illustration below by Dana Twigg*).

It's a common problem, actually. Animals get their heads stuck in empty containers more often than we realize. Discarded cups, bottles and jars are the primary cause, especially if they contain a sugary substance—raccoons and skunks being the primary victims.

Eager to get on with my patrol duty, I hurried back to my Bronco, opened the rear hatch, and took out a cardboard box used for transporting pint-sized critters, and a tackle box filled with syringes and tranquilizing paraphernalia designed for large mammals. The drug compound was a mixture of Rumpun and Ketamine, a muscle relaxing sedative commonly used on black bears and deer, but with a light dose, it is also effective on small mammals, especially skunks.

I had tranquilized a number of nuisance skunks over the years, but always by attaching the syringe to the end a four-foot-long aluminum pole designed to hold it in place. Then I would approach the skunk slowly, lower the syringe to its face and hold it there for a moment. Most skunks would sniff at the needle while keeping a wary eye on me. But because I would stand a relatively safe distance away and not make any sudden moves, they paid me little mind.

My next step was to move the syringe slowly past the unsuspecting skunk's head and ease the sharp needle slowly into its neck, pushing the syringe-pole forward one millimeter at a time. In seconds, the skunk would be immobilized and limp as a wet ragdoll, enabling me to pick it up and move the little critter into a box for safe transport to the nearest field or forest.

The problem with the skunk at hand was that he could not see me approach, because he was buried into a crevice up to his shoulders. My fear was that he'd let loose as soon as he felt my needle prick his skin. I had never injected a sedative into a skunk's rump before. Always the neck, ever so slowly, so he could see it coming and be unafraid. But I had no choice. I had to pull the skunk out of the stone crevice, and the only way to do that was by grabbing him by the back legs. The drug was my only hope. I'd been sprayed by a skunk once before on the trapline when I was a boy. Once was enough, and I didn't want it to happen again, especially while in full uniform in the middle of a busy deer season.

With much trepidation, I walked over to the skunk, took a syringe loaded with a small amount of sedative from my tackle box, and eased it into the skunk's rump. He never so much as twitched as I pulled the needle out and placed the syringe back in my tackle box. Being overly cautious, I waited a few minutes (even though the drug always acted instantly on skunks in the past) before taking hold of the stinker's hind legs and pulling him back out of the stone fissure. He was out cold, so I placed him into my cardboard box, carried everything back to my patrol car, and soon was on my way to Roaring Camp in Forkston Township. It was big woods country with plenty of open land where I released the skunk unharmed to sleep off the drugs along the way.

Roaring Camp was located along a remote dirt road in a heavily forested section of Wyoming County. I had received a number of anonymous reports concerning poaching activity stemming from the camp over the years but never came across anyone hunting unlawfully there.

But there's always a first time, and today was that day, for as I drove by the camp, I saw two freshly killed buck deer hanging from a meat pole out front. They were hung by their hind legs, side by side, heads close to the ground.

It's a routine practice of mine to inspect any deer I come across to be sure they are lawfully killed and properly tagged, so I pulled into a narrow dirt lane leading to the camp and parked by the deer.

As I approached the carcasses, two men dressed in camo orange walked out the front door of a prefabricated log cabin that was about a hundred feet away and hurried my way.

"Anything wrong?" one called out. He was of medium height with a stocky build. The other was much taller with a slender frame.

"State game warden," I said, turning toward them as they walked up to me. "Just a routine check of your deer."

"They're both tagged," insisted the slender man. "What's the problem?"

I could see each deer had a glossy big game tag attached to its ear as their heads dangled inches from the ground, but I wanted to be sure the tags were properly filled out. I crouched down and took a quick look. Although they had the sections requiring the hunters' name and address filled in, information regarding the points on each antler along with the date and location where the deer were killed, was left blank. Because it was early in the season, the tags could easily be used again and again over the next week or so.

I stood and faced the men. "What are your names?"

"I'm Gino," said the stocky man. He nodded at his partner. "This is my good friend, Tony. It's my camp. Tony is my guest."

"Your tags aren't properly filled out," I said. "I want to see some identification along with your hunting licenses."

Gino's tag. The township and date of kill were left blank.

Tony's tag. Township, date, time of kill, and antler points left blank.

Gino and Tony turned around so I could inspect the hunting licenses pinned to their coats. I removed each one from its plastic holder and pocketed them.

"You gonna keep our licenses?" cried Gino in surprise.

"For now," I said. "Let's see some ID to go along with them."

Gino pulled out his wallet and handed me a Pennsylvania driver's license. The information matched his hunting license, so I handed it back to him. I looked at Tony. "Where's yours?"

"It's in the cabin along with my wallet."

"Go get it."

Tony shook his head in disgust. "This is ridiculous!" he huffed. "I gave you my hunting license and my deer is tagged. Why are you harassing me?"

"You have a non-resident hunting license with a New Jersey address. It's a violation of our state Game Law not to completely fill out your tag. You can save yourself a lot of aggravation and get your driver's license for me. Otherwise, I'll have no choice but to place you under arrest and transport you to the local district justice."

"You can't be serious! You're gonna arrest me over a deer tag?"

"Only if you make me," I said.

Tony turned on his heels and stomped back to the cabin like a spoiled child who just lost his toy.

"I can't believe you're doing this!" Gino said angrily. "We tagged our deer. Why are you making a big issue out of it?"

"I think *you* are the one making a big issue out of this," I said. "You both filled out your tags with a ballpoint pen, probably after you brought them back to camp judging by how deep the printing looks. Am I right?"

"Yeah. Exactly. Right on the kitchen table."

"First, you're supposed to complete your tags immediately after killing a deer and before you transport the carcass in any manner. I'm okay with the fact that you didn't do that and took them to your camp first, but that also means you had plenty of time to do it properly by filling in all the information that's required, especially the date and time of kill."

Gino shrugged. "I forgot. It was just an oversight. Can't you give us a break?"

"That's one violation I never give breaks for. It's too easy to leave out critical information and then slip the tag in your pocket so you can use it on another deer. I've seen it happen too many times."

"But we weren't going to do that. Honest!"

"Everybody tells me that," I said, "but I'm not a mind reader. I don't know who's telling me the truth and who isn't, so I treat everyone the same. No breaks for untagged or improperly tagged deer."

I heard a door slam shut behind me and turned to see Tony coming toward us from the cabin: head down, shoulders hunched, feet pounding the ground. Obviously not in a good mood as he approached.

When he reached me, he thrust out a hand with his driver's license pinched between his thumb and forefinger. "Here!" he snapped at me.

I reached out to take it, but he held tight, refusing to let go.

"Give it to me," I said, opening my palm.

Tony dropped it on the ground instead. "Whoops!"

I glanced at Gino. He seemed to be sizing me up, wondering what I would do next, and I questioned whether they might suddenly turn on me if I displayed any sign of weakness.

"Pick it up and hand it to me" I said, "or I'm going to add littering and interfering with an officer to your list of violations."

Tony cocked his head toward Gino as if waiting for a sign of support for his roughish behavior.

Instead, Gino said, "Don't be a jerk, Tony. Give the man your license."

Tony rolled his eyes in disapproval, then he stooped down and picked up his license. "Here you go, warden," he said, handing it to me.

I looked it over carefully and dropped it in my coat pocket.

"Hey! What did you do that for?" Tony cried. "I have to drive back to Jersey tonight, and I need that."

"You're not going anywhere until we get this settled," I told him. "The fine is one hundred dollars for your tagging violation. That goes for you, too, Gino."

"That's ridiculous!" scoffed Gino. "My deer was tagged; I just forgot to fill out the date."

"You can tell your story to a judge or settle with me today on a field acknowledgment of guilt. It's your call."

Gino thought for a moment, then: "Simple enough. I'll see you in court."

"Me too," said Tony.

It's a different matter for you," I said to him. "Gino is a Pennsylvania resident, he can wait. You live out of state, which means you'll have to see a judge today."

Tony shook his head in disapproval. "No way. That doesn't give me enough time to find a lawyer."

"You have two choices: settle on a field acknowledgment of guilt and pay now, or I'll take you in for an immediate hearing with a judge. You can't go back to New Jersey unless the judge finds you not guilty or you post bail for a hearing at a later date."

Tony's face turned red as he launched into a tirade about how stupid the law was and how absurd I was being for enforcing it. Finally, he paused, venom in his eyes. "Fine!" he squealed; his voice hoarse from his ranting. "Take me to a judge right now! I demand to have my day in court!"

I led Tony to my patrol car and sat him in the front passenger seat. Game Commission patrol cars didn't have a protective barrier behind the front seat to safely transport prisoners like other police cars, so I had no choice but to keep him up front with me. I had grown tired of his arrogant behavior by now. It was buck season, and I had four hundred square miles to patrol, so I wanted to get this over with and move on, but Gino and Tony had kept chipping away at me, dragging out the process. There was no doubt in my mind that the men intended to use their tags over again. They got caught, plain and simple. But instead of behaving like adults and paying their fines, they had to rant and rave as if it were my fault for doing my job and enforcing the law.

The Game Commission didn't require deer hunters to bring their kills into check stations like bear hunters. With a million deer hunters scattered all over the state, we simply didn't have the manpower to place employees at locations in all sixty-seven counties in order to accommodate them. Instead, we had to rely on our tagging system along with the requirement that all hunters fill out a harvest report card issued with their hunting license after killing their deer and mail it to the Game Commission. Most hunters obeyed our tagging laws, but the few who didn't had to be prosecuted, otherwise, the word would spread that game wardens were giving breaks for improperly tagged deer, which would entice more dishonest hunters to violate an important law.

On the way to the district justice's office, I radioed into Wyoming County Communications asking them to contact the judge and let her know that I was on my way to her courtroom with a non-resident hunter who had demanded an immediate trial. They radioed back that the judge for that area was not available (because it was a Saturday, most courts were closed) and that the duty magistrate was leaving her office at noon.

Had Tony been more cooperative and respectful, I might have simply issued him a citation and went on my way, trusting that he would do the right thing and pay his fine or return to Pennsylvania for a hearing at a later date. But Tony didn't seem like that kind of guy, and unlike Gino, who filled out everything on his tag except the township and date of kill (which might have garnered him a not guilty verdict in front of a sympathetic judge), Tony only entered the county of kill on his tag, leaving everything else blank. He was wasting his time with a hearing and should have had enough sense to realize that.

Besides, I knew that the duty magistrate had a background in hunting and would find him guilty. She had done it time and again with other hunters. But I couldn't tell Tony that; I knew he would only use my words against me and accuse me of forcing him to settle on a field acknowledgement rather than have a fair trial in front of an impartial judge. Don't get me wrong, the judge was fair with every defendant. But she also followed the law to the letter. And in this case, the law was quite simple: you must fill out your deer tag *completely* or pay a hundred dollar fine.

Although I thought Tony was a jerk, I also didn't think it was fair to leave him languishing in jail for who knows how long over a tagging violation, which was his only choice if we didn't get to the judge's office quickly. We didn't have much time; it was eleven o'clock and Roaring Camp was miles away in a remote section of the county, so I was moving along at the maximum speed limit for the road when Tony began to complain.

"I still can't believe you're making a big deal out of this," he said. "My deer was tagged, and I had no intention of using the tag again."

"You can tell your story to the judge. We'll see what she has to say."

"I'm going to do just that. I promise you."

"Okay," I said.

"You're driving too fast."

"No, I'm not."

"Yes, you are."

"I'm going fifty-five. That's not too fast."

"No citation is worth my life. I want you to slow down!"

I'd had about enough of Tony at this point. Here I was, trying to help the guy stay out of jail, and he was being ridiculous. "You need to just sit still and shut up," I said heatedly.

Suddenly, Tony snapped. "Nobody talks to me like that!" he shouted as he unbuckled his seatbelt and hurled it toward the passenger window.

I quickly grabbed his shoulder with my right hand and slammed him against the passenger door, pinning him there as I pulled to the shoulder and stopped. "Get out of the car!" I commanded.

Tony opened the door and stepped out while I quickly walked around to face him. I never should have left him in my car without cuffing him. It was a mistake on my part.

"Turn around and put your hands behind your back," I told him.

Tony complied, and I pulled a set of handcuffs from my duty belt and shackled him before continuing to the district courthouse.

Judge Patricia Robinson walked into the courtroom through a doorway to our left as Tony and I rose from our chairs in mutual respect for her office. She stepped over to her desk in front of us, sat down, and began to examine the citation I had placed on her desk as Tony and I took our seats. It spelled out the charge against my defendant, and after reviewing it carefully, she read the charge aloud and asked Tony how he would plea.

"Not guilty," he replied. "And this officer never should have—"

"Excuse me," interrupted the judge. "You'll get your chance to testify, but not until you're sworn in and Officer Wasserman presents his case against you. Understood?"

Tony shrugged lazily. "I guess so."

The judge glanced at me with questioning eyes, *where did this rube come from?*

I rolled my eyes in return. Tony was off to a great start with the judge. Yes indeed.

"Are you ready to proceed?" she asked me.

"Yes, Your Honor."

The judge swore me in, and I took a seat in the witness chair next to her desk. Reaching into my shirt pocket, I pulled out Tony's deer tag and handed it to her.

"This is the defendant's deer tag," I began. "It was attached to a five-point buck hanging from a pole at Roaring Camp in Forkston Township. The defendant, who is seated directly in front of you, admitted killing the deer." Next, I handed her Tony's hunting license. "As you can see, the number on the hunting license matches the number on the tag."

She paused and looked over both items. "I see the defendant is from New Jersey," she said.

"Correct, Your Honor. Which is why he requested an immediate hearing."

"Proceed," she said.

From there, I explained how I stopped to inspect two deer hanging at Roaring Camp and found that both were improperly tagged. At that point I was confronted by Tony and Gino. I told her about Tony's poor behavior, that he did not want to settle on a field acknowledgement of guilt and that I didn't believe he would return to Pennsylvania if I handed him a citation.

"He's a liar!" shouted Tony. "He's the one who—"

The judge picked up a wooden gavel and rapped it on her desk. "That's enough!" she warned. "You'll get your chance to testify, but I don't want to hear any more outbursts from you."

Judge Robinson looked over at me. "Do you have any further testimony?"

"No, Your Honor."

Tony took the stand next and told his side of the story. According to him, I was the one who exhibited bad behavior. He went on to claim that I shouldn't have examined his deer because I didn't knock at the cabin and ask first, and I didn't have permission to be on the property, nor did I have a search warrant. He also complained that my stop at the camp was nothing more than harassment because I could see from the road that both deer had tags attached to their ears, but that I decided to meddle by walking across private property to make sure every little space on the tag was filled in. "That's just wrong!" he complained, pointing a finger at me. "Gino and I were having a great time until this guy showed up. We both killed a nice buck early that morning, and we were inside celebrating by a warm fire when we saw the warden's truck pull into our property, which is posted against trespassing."

He went on to argue that the United States Constitution provided that he and Gino were free from unreasonable searches and seizures, and that they had an expectation of privacy on their clearly posted property. Then he argued that the tag I submitted as evidence should be suppressed due to the lack of a search warrant.

"And when this trial is over," he added, "I'm going to file charges against the game warden for trespassing on our land and for violating my constitutional rights!"

Judge Robinson asked if Tony had anything further to say, and he declined.

Turning to me she asked, "Do you have questions for the defendant?'

"No further questions, Your Honor. I believe the tag I submitted for evidence is sufficient for a conviction. I do, however, have a closing statement."

"Proceed," she said.

I stood from my chair and argued that Section 901 of the Pennsylvania Game Law states that any officer whose duty it is to investigate any alleged violations of the Law shall have the power and duty to go upon any land, outside of buildings, posted or otherwise, in the performance of his duty. As a result, I did not need a search warrant to enter posted property. His cabin, certainly. But not his property.

Tony surprised me by arguing that although the Game Law granted wardens the right to search private property without a warrant, he maintained that to do so was a violation of his constitutional right to privacy by virtue of the United States Constitution. And that because the Constitution superseded state laws, my warrantless search was unlawful. He insisted therefore, that all evidence against him should be thrown out and the case against him dismissed.

Judge Robinson considered Tony's argument, then asked, "Didn't you just testify that Officer Wasserman could see both deer were tagged from the road?"

"That's right. And he should have kept on driving instead of trespassing on private property."

"That's your opinion, sir," she said. "But game wardens do have the right, under the Game Law, to enter private property, even if it's posted. The deer, by your own admission, were in plain view, close to the road. The officer didn't search your cabin or the area immediately around your cabin, so there was no violation of your constitutional right to privacy. Therefore, I find you guilty as charged."

(Little did I know that years later, this same argument regarding search and seizure on private property would go all the way to the Pennsylvania Supreme Court in a bear baiting case that I brought before Judge Robinson. Their conclusion was as follows: *The citizens of this Commonwealth throughout our history have shown a keen interest in protecting and preserving the diverse wildlife that find refuge in the fields and forests within our borders. This interest is so strong that it is enshrined by a separate provision of the Pennsylvania Constitution.*

The legislative and executive branches, in turn, have enacted and executed a plethora of statutes and regulations designed to enforce the people's right to the preservation of our wildlife. Thus, our Constitution and enacted statutes — as well as the agencies created to enforce them — all confirm that, in Pennsylvania, any subjective expectation for privacy against governmental intrusion in open fields is not an expectation that our society has ever been willing to recognize as reasonable.

Tony turned beet red before exploding into an abusive outburst. "I knew it!" he shouted. "First, I get arrested by some backwoods warden who thinks he's John Wayne, and then he takes me to Hillbilly Central for a hearing in a kangaroo court! I'm going to appeal this ridiculous show trial in front of a real judge. I can guarantee you that!"

Judge Robinson kept her cool. I knew she was upset by what Tony said. Any decent judge would be. But she never displayed a hint of anger, refusing to give him the satisfaction of ruffling her feathers.

"You have the right to appeal my decision before the county appellate court," she said. "But for now, you must pay the fine and costs for this violation or post bail in the same amount before I can let you go."

Tony shook his head in disgust. "How much is it?"

"The fine is one hundred dollars plus twenty-five dollars in court costs."

"Outrageous," he muttered, reaching into his back pocket for a wallet. But his face suddenly turned white when he discovered it wasn't there. Tony started patting his other pockets, searching for his wallet in a wild frenzy. He grabbed his coat off the back of his chair and patted it down frantically, hoping to find it there. Finally, he looked up at the judge, hopelessness in his eyes. "I must have left it back at camp."

"Then you'll have to wait in the county jail until someone comes up with the money," she replied.

Tony knew he was at her mercy. He didn't dare argue. "But we don't have a phone at camp," he pleaded. "I won't be able to call Gino and have him bring my wallet."

Judge Robinson glanced at a wall clock to her right. "I don't have any more time for this today. I have no choice but to draw up the commitment papers and have Officer Wasserman take you to the county jail."

The judge really didn't want to put the man in jail, but she didn't know what else to do at this point.

"Your Honor," I said. "I'll drive the defendant back to camp if he agrees to settle on a field acknowledgement of guilt. That will keep him out of jail, and we can all be on our way, if that's okay with you."

She looked at the defendant. "Are you agreeable to these terms?"

"Under the circumstances, I am most agreeable," he said.

Tony never stopped yapping away as we headed for Roaring Camp along Route 6. It was a beautiful state road passing through some of the best deer hunting within the Endless Mountain Region of northeast Pennsylvania. Along the way, we saw dozens of vehicles parked by the road that belonged to deer hunters. In the distance, armies of orange-clad men pushed through the open woods, hoping to drive a trophy buck into the shooting range of awaiting hunters.

"I guess those poor suckers will be your next victims,"

Tony said bitterly.

"Those handcuffs aren't too tight, are they?" I replied, ignoring his remark.

"Like you care, right?"

I don't think I ever met a man who was more ungrateful than Tony. If it weren't for my suggestion to have him settle on a field acknowledgement, he'd be sitting in jail right now. I couldn't help but think that *I* was the sucker, not the hunters he had just referred to. Maybe jail would have been the best place for him. Then I would've been free of him and out on patrol like I should've been. But I couldn't see incarcerating the man for a minor Game Law violation and had hoped my solution to that impending major inconvenience for him might have softened his temperament.

It did not.

"How does this field acknowledgment of guilt thing work?" he asked.

"I have official state documents with me where I write down the violation and the section of law that applies to it. Then you sign it and pay the fine to settle the case."

"Do you take credit cards?"

"Cash only," I said.

"How about a check?"

"No checks."

"So, I hand you a hundred dollars cash and you drive off into the sunset, right? No wonder you're running around handing out tickets for everything you can think of. Good way to make some extra cash, huh?"

"I don't keep the money. It's turned over to the Game Commission."

"How do they know you're not pocketing it?"

"It's called honesty, Tony. Something you need to work on yourself."

When I reached Roaring Camp, I parked next to the meat pole where Gino and Tony's deer were hanging and got Tony out of my vehicle. As I was removing his handcuffs, Gino came out the front door of the cabin and approached.

"What's this?" he cried. "You got handcuffs on my friend! He doesn't deserve that!"

"Standard procedure," I told him. "Nothing personal."

Gino looked at Tony. "Everything okay?"

Tony shook his head. "Not really. The judge found me guilty and was going to throw me in jail if I didn't pay or post bail. But I forgot my wallet, so now I have to pay the warden a hundred dollar fine to stay out of jail."

"Okay, so pay the man and let him go on his way. We still have men out there, and they want to put on another drive before dark." He looked at me. "We can still participate in a drive if we're unarmed, right?"

"Yes, just be sure to have your hunting license on your back and wear orange clothing."

Gino glared at Tony. "Come on, Tony. Step it up. Get your wallet and give the man his money."

I thought it odd that Gino seemed in a big hurry for me to leave. I still had his hunting license in my pocket from earlier in the day and he didn't ask for it, even though I just told him he had to have it with him to drive deer. And there was something else: he looked nervous, his eyes flitting about as if waiting for someone to jump out of the bushes and attack him.

"Can I appeal my acknowledgement of guilt after I sign the document?" asked Tony.

"I don't think so," I said. "I never heard of anyone doing that before."

Tony frowned. "That's the only reason I agreed to do this. You should have told me that before we left the judge's office."

"You should have asked." I said.

Gino grabbed Tony by the shoulder and spun him around. "We're going into the cabin to get your money right now. Stop arguing with the man. I know a good attorney and I'm sure he'll be able to help us. Now let's go!"

There was no doubt in my mind that things had changed at Roaring Camp in the last two hours. Gino looked frazzled. His face was white, and his hands trembled. He wanted to get rid of me as soon as possible. I watched as he wrapped an arm around Tony and ushered him toward their cabin. He was talking to him in low tones, his words fast and breathless.

When they disappeared into the cabin, I scanned the immediate area for any sign of foul play. But there was nothing that seemed out of place. There were five pickup trucks parked by the cabin, so I walked over and looked in their beds thinking an illegal doe might be lying inside one of them. Again, nothing to see. Not even a drop of blood to indicate a deer had been transported.

I didn't have a search warrant, or even a good reason to get one, so there wasn't much more I could do. Buck season was heating up. I could hear shots in the distance indicating a number of hunters had found their mark. The best I could do would be to come back later in the day, so long as I didn't get tied up with another case.

I was on my way back to my patrol car to grab some paperwork for Tony's acknowledgment of guilt when the two cups of coffee I had earlier in the morning suddenly triggered an urgency for me to find relief. There was a clapboard outhouse at the edge of the woods, so I started hustling toward it when Gino ran out of the cabin.

"Don't go in there!" he hollered. "It's closed for repairs."

I kept walking. *What repairs?* I thought. The structure looked perfect: hardly used and freshly painted in a rustic shade of woodsy brown.

Within seconds, I realized why Gino didn't want me anywhere near the structure. As I got closer, I saw a matted area in the grass indicating that a deer had been dragged from the woods directly to the outhouse.

I turned around and saw Gino and Tony coming toward me in a hurry, so I stopped and waited for them. "You can't go in there," insisted Gino. "The floor is rotted and it's not safe."

Tony said, "I have a hundred dollars in my pocket and I'm ready to settle. I know you're in a hurry to get back on patrol, so let's get this over with."

"Buck or doe?" I asked.

Gino and Tony exchanged tense looks. "What are you talking about?" asked Gino.

"I know you have a deer inside the outhouse." I pointed to the matted swath in the grass. "I can see where someone dragged it in there from the woods. Is it a buck or a doe?"

"Gino puffed his cheeks and blew a heavy sigh. "Okay. I admit it. There's a doe inside. But Tony and I had nothing to do with it."

"Bring it out here," I said.

Gino stepped over to the outhouse, opened the door and dragged out a small doe that had been gutted. The carcass looked to be about eighty pounds.

"Whose deer is it?" I said.

"Bruno killed it," said Gino. "He was dragging it out of the woods when he saw your patrol car pull into our property this morning. He waited until you left with Tony and then he ran out of the woods and told me he killed a doe. He said it was an accident. I told him you were coming back, and that he should report it, but he said he wanted to keep it. It was his brilliant idea to hide it in the outhouse, thinking you wouldn't see it."

"Where is Bruno now?" I asked.

"He's in the cabin. Probably watching us."

"Go get him."

While waiting for Bruno to come out of the cabin and show himself, I dragged the small doe over to my patrol car and put it on my big game carrier at the rear bumper. I only knew of one other man named Bruno, and I envisioned a hulking, barrel-chested giant like the famed 1960s world wrestling champion Bruno Sammartino. My brother and I loved to watch the Wide World Wrestling Federation's professional wrestlers do battle on TV when we were young. Sammartino was our hero. He was always a gentleman and was the reigning world heavyweight champion for more than seven consecutive years.

But Bruno the deer slayer from Roaring Camp wasn't big

at all. In fact, he only outweighed the illegal doe he killed by twenty pounds or so. Bruno was all of five-foot-four inches tall and skinny as a rail as he shuffled over to my patrol car and handed me his hunting license. His address showed that he lived in the same town as Gino.

"I'm sorry, officer," he said. "It was an accident. I thought I saw horns, but when I walked over to gut it out, I discovered it was a doe. The deer was in the brush, under some low branches that made it look like it had antlers. Gino told me the fine is a hundred dollars. I'm ready to pay."

"You have to make an effort to report an accidentally killed deer to the Game Commission," I said. "You can't hide it in an outhouse and expect leniency. You're looking at a five-hundred dollar fine, not a hundred."

Bruno swallowed hard. "You gotta be kidding! That's a lot of money!"

"It's supposed to be," I said.

The incident at Roaring Camp didn't end that day. Gino and Bruno both paid their fines in full and never did hire an attorney to fight the charges. Although Tony did settle on a field acknowledgment and paid a one hundred dollar fine, he wrote a blistering letter to my supervisor, Barry Warner, accusing me of physical and verbal abuse both while conducting my investigation and while he was being transported to the judge's office. Warner questioned me about the incident and also paid a visit to Judge Robinson's office to hear what she had to say. The judge explained that had I not offered to take Tony back to camp so he could settle on a field acknowledgment, she would have sent him to the county jail.

After his investigation into the affair, Warner wrote a letter to Tony stating that the judge told him that he had been argumentative throughout his stay in her office, and that in her opinion, the game warden went out of his way to help him by taking him back to camp for money to settle the case. Warner ended his letter by stating that the matter was closed and there would be no further action on his behalf.

Still, Tony persisted by writing another letter, this time to Dick Fagan, Chief of Law Enforcement in Harrisburg. Mr. Fagan looked into the matter and wrote back to Tony. His final words were: "You violated the law, had your day in court and justice was served."

None but the well-bred man knows how to confess a fault or acknowledge himself in an error.
~Benjamin Franklin

Shoot First

JAYSON AND HIS SON KYLE had looked forward to the first day of spring gobbler season for many months until it finally arrived. And it was early in the morning as they sat side-by-side in the dark, their backs against a towering oak, as Kyle's father pulled a wooden box call from his coat pocket. Kyle was twelve years old, and it was the first time he'd ever been hunting.

It was one of those clear, calm high-pressure mornings when sound traveled. Jayson knew his calls would sound true and carry far.

"The sun will be up soon," Jason whispered to his son. "You have to be real quiet while I work this call."

Kyle looked up at his father and nodded that he understood.

"If you see a turkey coming our way, wait until he's in range," added Jason. "Thirty-five yards or closer before you shoot."

"Okay," whispered Kyle.

Kyle's heart began to pound so hard he could hear it. He thought the sound might scare a turkey away, so he tried to relax, tried to control his excitement, but to no avail. He couldn't wait to see a turkey and hoped it would be a big tom strutting right at him with its tail all fanned out. Kyle had pictured the image in his mind every day for weeks and hoped it would soon be a reality.

In the distance, maybe a hundred and fifty yards or so, he

could hear a turkey gobbling like crazy. He looked up at his father, eyes questioning why he didn't start working his box call.

His father held a finger to his lips. "Shhh," he whispered. "When the sky starts to turn pink, I'll call him in."

Kyle nodded, then turned his head toward the distant hollow where the gobbling was coming from, his eyes boring into the fading darkness as he watched and waited for the turkey to finally appear.

Jimmy Jones had a late start that morning. He couldn't believe his alarm clock didn't go off. Next time he'd make sure the batteries were fresh. It was still dark as he raced toward his favorite hollow in anticipation of a successful morning. Jimmy was an experienced hunter and had killed his share of turkeys over the years. Jimmy also hunted over bait whenever he could, which was one of the reasons he was so successful every spring and fall. The chopped corn and milo he'd been spreading around the hollow for the past month was sure to lure in a bunch of turkeys. In fact, if he was lucky and they were packed tight over the bait, he might even hit two birds with one shot.

The hollow was along a stretch of road only ten miles from his house, and with his foot pressed heavy on the gas pedal, he managed to get there in a matter of minutes.

Jimmy parked his pickup truck along a grassy berm at the edge of the road and jumped out the door. The sky was illuminated with a pink glow as he started down the hollow with his shotgun in hand. If there were turkeys working the bait, he'd scare them off. But they'd be back. No question about it.

But aside from being a poacher, Jimmy had other faults, and one of them was his extreme lack of patience, which is why he hunted over bait. It was never about the hunt with Jimmy; it was always about the kill. And along with it came the bragging rights. Jimmy loved to boast about his skill as a hunter at the local tavern. He was a loner and had no friends, so he would go to the bar and drink every night, imagining the customers gathered inside were impressed with his stories. In truth, none of them were impressed at all, and most suspected he was poaching game.

Unfortunately, no one ever bothered to call the game warden and tip him off about their suspicions.

Long before Jimmy reached the hollow, the gobbler that Kyle and his father were calling flew off its limb and ran the other way. Jimmy could have eased his door closed when he hopped out of the truck. But he was in a hurry and swung the door a little too hard. That was all it took for the wary gobbler to head for parts unknown.

When he reached his bait station, he concealed himself behind the blind he'd built of brush and saplings earlier in the year. He was about to settle in for a while when he heard a series of clucks and yelps coming from a hen turkey. She was fairly close, maybe two hundred yards or so away, near the ridge top.

Why sit here and wait when there's a turkey begging to be shot? he thought. It was a long season and there would be plenty of opportunities to kill more birds. Jimmy decided to move in on the hen and shoot her. The fact that hen turkeys were illegal during spring gobbler season and that hunting by stalking was also prohibited played in his mind, but he quickly shrugged it off. Who would know? The game warden had an entire county to patrol, and Jimmy could be back to his truck and home with his kill in minutes. The odds were in his favor. Besides, for all he knew, the warden wasn't even out of bed yet.

In the distance there came a cluck, yelp, and a purr. Jimmy began to move in.

Kyle's father continued to work his box call even though the tom had stopped gobbling. Jayson was a patient man and didn't try to push the gobbler too hard. He knew that too much calling early in the morning could make a turkey hang back on its limb waiting for the hen to walk under his roost tree. His plan was to cluck and yelp a little louder so the gobbler would focus its attention in his direction, but he didn't want to overdo it and spook the bird. He knew that some toms were slow to go and might take thirty minutes or more before coming in to his call.

Kyle didn't have the patience of his father. His heart was hammering with excitement, and his eyes flicked from tree to tree hoping to see a gobbler magically appear from behind one of them. Jayson looked down at his son and smiled. He remembered his first hunt with his own father so many years ago. He remembered how excited he was and how hunting with his father had brought them closer. And he remembered how much he loved his father and how it had hurt him when he passed away. Jayson wanted that same closeness with Kyle. That same bond of love. And his heart swelled with joy just knowing his son was here with him, sharing in the excitement of the hunt.

Jayson worked his call again: three sultry clucks, when Kyle suddenly spotted a shadowy figure in the distance. A fleeting movement to his right that emerged from behind a tree. It crept toward them, low to the ground. He glanced up at his father; he was looking straight ahead and didn't see it. Kyle gripped hold of his shotgun as a coyote suddenly appeared from the shadows A big one too, coming straight toward them quiet as a ghost. Frightened that they were about to be gobbled up by the wolflike creature, he nudged his father with an elbow and nodded toward the advancing predator.

Jayson acted immediately. He'd heard of coyotes pouncing on camouflaged hunters who were calling spring gobblers thinking they were hens. It was rare, but it did happen. Not wanting to risk injury to either of them, Jayson grabbed the orange hat hidden between his knees and waved it in the air. That was all it took. The frightened coyote pivoted so fast it almost turned inside out before dashing back into the brush, never to be seen again.

Jayson looked down at his son and gave him a reassuring

smile. Kyle's eyes were filled with apprehension and wonder.

"He won't' be back," his father whispered. And he began to work his box call once more. A few clucks, a putt, and a purr.

Jimmy Jones envisioned the stares of wide-eyed admiration he'd receive from his buddies at the bar when he made up a story transforming the hen he was about to kill into a trophy gobbler. Slowly and methodically, he moved toward Jayson's call with cautious, almost fluid precision. A lifetime of poaching had taught him to be deadly silent in the woods.

He was close now. Very close. The soft purrs and clucks had come from between a large white oak and a stand of scrub brush forty yards ahead. He froze, eyes boring into the brush for a glimpse of his prize as he slowly brought his Ithaca pump gun to his shoulder. There would be no problem hitting it through the brush, his ten-gauge shotgun packed a mean wallop to be sure. With his finger on the trigger, he would be quick to squeeze off a shot at first sight of the bird.

There! Something moved behind the brush! Jimmy squeezed off a round, shooting directly at it.

He heard a scream. Then another. Human voices? Impossible!

He ran toward them. In seconds he was there. A man and a boy! How could it be?

Young Kyle was sitting on the ground holding his face in his hands. His father stood to his feet as Jimmy approached.

"What are you shooting at?" Jayson shouted angrily. "You hit both of us. Are you crazy?"

Jimmy was in shock. He couldn't believe he just shot two hunters in mistake for a turkey. The man was bleeding from a hole in his cheek and another in his lip. The boy looked up at him. He'd been hit in the face too. Jimmy could see pellet wounds in his left eyebrow and the bridge of his nose. He could have been blinded, he thought.

His stomach wrenched into a knot and he felt his chest tighten. He'd been hunting (mostly poaching) for forty years.

How could he have mistaken them for a turkey? But Jimmy's concern was more about himself than it was his two victims. The most important thing right now was to think of a way to get out of this jam he'd put himself into. His mind began to race: the injuries looked serious, and one of them was only a boy. Hospital bills, lawsuits, game law penalties, loss of his hunting license, attorney fees. The list never ended.

Suddenly it came to him. A lifetime of poaching had taught him to be a master of deceit. "I've hunted gobblers here since I've been six," he told Jayson. "I shot at one and didn't see you. I'm sorry."

"That was *me* you shot at. There was no gobbler here!"

"I'm telling you there was!" insisted Jimmy. "It was on my side of the brush, and I couldn't see you when I shot at it."

Jayson had no time to argue with him. "Turn around and show me your hunting license," he demanded.

Jimmy complied and Jayson wrote the number on the palm of his hand with a pen he'd brought to fill out his turkey tag. There was a gas station a few miles away. They would have a phone. "I'm going to call for an ambulance," he said to Jimmy. "My son is injured a lot worse than me. I'd advise you to stick around. I have your license number and I'll be calling the game warden too."

Wyoming County Police Communications contacted me by radio within minutes after Jayson called nine-one-one for the ambulance. They knew to report all hunting related shooting incidents to the Game Commission right away, and because I happened to be on patrol in the immediate area, I arrived with a deputy before the ambulance got there.

Jayson and Kyle were in mild pain, but both were in good spirits when we arrived and didn't mind talking to us while waiting for the ambulance. Jayson told me he was calling a tom they had heard gobbling when a single shot rang out with pellets striking both of them. He explained that Jimmy Jones admitted firing the shot, claiming he was shooting at a turkey and never saw them. Jayson had one pellet lodged in his right cheek and another in his upper lip. Another pellet struck the underside of is left forearm causing a noticeable bruise. Kyle was hit with six pellets in his right thigh, causing five bruises and one entry wound. Three pellets struck the back of his right hand with two causing bruises and the third lodging deep into his flesh. He also had one pellet enter the flesh under his left eyebrow and another entry wound to the right side of his nose. Arrows point to the wounds described above.

About the time I finished interviewing Jayson and his son, the ambulance arrived and took both victims to Tyler Memorial Hospital, so I turned my investigation toward Jimmy Jones.

Jimmy insisted that he was shooting at a turkey with a four-inch beard and that he could not see Jayson or his son. My deputy and I looked around and could not see any scratchings, tracks or other signs of a turkey. When I asked where he was when he shot at the turkey, he pointed in a direction that didn't correspond with the shot pattern that struck Jayson and Kyle. Because Jimmy was not cooperating, my deputy and I searched the area until we found a freshly fired shotgun shell from a ten-gauge shotgun. It matched the ammo that Jimmy had in his pockets. From there, we traced the zone of fire directly to where Jayson and Kyle had been by marking trees struck by pellets from Jimmy's blast.

Deputy points to pellets lodged in sapling.

We followed the zone of fire for 133 feet, sticking a piece of white paper into each pellet hole on every tree that was hit. We also photographed everything. There were injuries to both hunters, and we expected a court trial and wanted to be sure there was sufficient evidence for a successful prosecution.

Tree marked with white paper showing pellet holes from blast.

Although we had built a substantial case against Jimmy Jones, I wanted a confession to seal the deal.

"Is that your blue Ford pickup parked by the road?" I asked.

Jimmy nodded that it was.

"I'm parked behind you," I said. "Come with me; I've got paperwork to do."

I wanted Jimmy seated in my patrol car when I questioned him about the shooting. I had my briefcase and citation pad in the car and intended to file charges against him before my deputy and I went to the hospital to interview the two victims.

Jimmy shadowed me to my vehicle while my deputy trailed behind him. When we arrived, I searched him for hidden weapons before opening the passenger door so he could get in.

"Am I under arrest?" he asked nervously.

"No. I have a few more questions to ask. That's all."

Jimmy crawled inside and sat in the passenger seat, and I shut the door behind him. Turning to my deputy, I motioned for him to start scouting the area before I slid inside with Jimmy.

"Do you know about your right to remain silent?" I asked.

Jimmy stared out the windshield and shrugged. "Heard about it. They do it on cop shows sometimes."

I pulled a card from my wallet with the Miranda Warning inscribed on it. "Well, here it is for real," I said, and began to read: *You have the right to remain silent. Anything you say can be used against you in court. You have the right to talk to a lawyer for advice before I ask you any questions. You have the right to have a lawyer with you during questioning. If you decide to answer questions now without a lawyer present, you have the right to stop answering at any time.*

I stuffed the card back in my wallet. "Do you want to talk?"

"Sure," he said. "It was an accident. Like I told you before: I never saw them sitting behind the brush. They didn't have any orange clothing. If they did, I would have seen them, and I wouldn't have taken the shot."

Jimmy looked out the side window of my patrol car and saw my deputy heading into the woods. "Where's he going?" There was alarm in his voice.

"Foot patrol," I said. "Why?"

"He's gonna scare all the gobblers away."

"I think that already happened when the ambulance arrived."

"Why isn't he in a uniform like you. You *look* like a game warden. He looks like a hunter."

"Exactly," I said.

Jimmy nodded thoughtfully. "I get it. So he can creep up on hunters, right? Pretty sneaky if you ask me."

"That's not one of the questions I want to ask you right now."

"What then?" Jimmy complained. "What do you want from me?"

"The truth."

"I told you already. I saw a—"

"Stop it!" I barked, cutting him off. "We traced your shot pattern directly to Jayson and Kyle. You told us you were shooting in a different direction. You lied. And there is no sign that a turkey had been there. Besides, don't you think they would have noticed a gobbler coming to their call?"

Jimmy stared down at the floor and shook his head somberly. "You're right. I can't believe I shot them," he said. "Forty-five years hunting in the woods, and I shoot somebody in mistake for a turkey. I ain't gonna lie to you no more. I did it. I saw movement behind the brush and thought I saw a turkey back there, so I shot."

I asked Jimmy if he would give me a written statement and he agreed, so I pulled a blank document for that purpose from my briefcase, handed him a pen, and watched as he scrawled his confession for me.

At about the same time that Jimmy finished writing his confession, my deputy came walking out of the woods with a small plastic evidence bag in his hand. I told Jimmy to sit tight while I exited my vehicle and walked over to meet him.

"What do you have?" I asked.

"Cracked corn. I saw some kernels in the bed of this truck, so I walked straight into the woods and found a bunch of it scattered a few hundred yards back in the hollow. Found a blind too. Looks like Jimmy was planning to hunt over bait when he heard Jayson's box call."

"Good job," I said. "Now all I have to do is get him to admit the bait was his."

"Shouldn't be too hard," said my deputy as he reached into a pocket and handed me a clear plastic bag with two spent ten-gauge shotgun shells inside. Both were red 3 ½-inch casings marked as number four shot and identical to the ammo Jimmy was using when he shot Jayson and Kyle. "They're fresh, too," added my deputy. "Haven't been lying around too long."

"Did you find any sign of turkeys being shot?" I asked.

"I think so. I circled the area until I found two possible locations. A few feathers was all, about ten yards apart and thirty yards from the blind."

Jimmy looked worried when I walked back to my patrol car and slid inside next to him. "Is that your blind down in the woods?" I asked.

"What blind?"

"And the cracked corn? Is that yours too?"

"I don't know what you're talking about."

I reached into my coat pocket and pulled out the plastic bag with two shotgun shells inside. "Recognize these?"

"Should I?"

"They're the same as the ones you have on you today. Exactly the same."

"So? Everybody hunts turkeys with shotguns."

"Mostly twelve-gauge shotguns," I said. "Not tens."

Jimmy shrugged and looked away from me.

"I'm going to the State Police Crime Lab in Kingston to have the shell you shot Jayson and Kyle with matched to your shotgun. It's a simple matter to have the two shells my deputy found matched too."

"Matched?"

"Yep. Their lab technicians use a special microscope to locate digital images of the firing pin impression, the breech face, and the ejector mark on a firearm against a cartridge case. It's as good as finding fingerprints on the gun that fired the rounds. Any court in the land will accept these findings as evidence that a specific cartridge was fired from a specific gun."

Jimmy weighed what I said for a moment. Then: "So, maybe I was shooting at squirrels or something."

I said, "My deputy found signs near the blind indicating that two turkeys were killed. Maybe you were shooting at turkeys."

Jimmy turned away and stared out the passenger window of my patrol car. "Can I go now?"

"No, you cannot. I'm going to send my deputy into Tunkhannock for a search warrant. It'll take a while, but when he comes back, we're going to search your house, garage, outbuildings vehicles and anything else on your property for the turkeys you killed. When we find them, I'm going to charge you with everything in the book. And when I'm done, you're going to lose your hunting license for at least ten years."

"Ten years?"

"At least."

Jimmy swallowed hard.

I waited for a long moment. Then: "It doesn't have to be that way."

Jimmy looked at me with a questioning brow.

"It's the first day of spring gobbler season," I said. "I have a hunting accident to clear up and about a million other things I could be doing rather than sit around waiting for my deputy to return with a search warrant. Cooperation on your part will go a long way, a very long way in fact, toward a reduction on the poaching charges I could file against you."

Jimmy nodded that he understood. "What exactly are you asking for?"

"A signed Consent to Search document permitting my deputy and me to search your property."

"And I get what?"

"Depends on what we find."

"What if I have two turkeys in my chest freezer? That's it. Nothing else?"

"If that's the case, two charges for killing turkeys in closed season over bait. No additional charges for unlawful transportation, tagging, or hunting from a blind. There will also be charges for shooting a human in mistake for game, but that was going to happen anyway and has nothing to do with the two turkeys you say you have in your freezer. In other words, your cooperation will save you about a thousand dollars in fines."

Jimmy thought for a moment. "Fair enough, I guess," he finally replied.

Jimmy Jones lived in a small, single-story wood framed house nestled in the woods along a seldom-traveled dirt road in Meshoppen Township. I parked my patrol car directly behind his Ford pickup when he pulled into a two-track driveway leading to his house and exited his vehicle. The place needed a lot of work, especially the roof, which seemed to sag somewhat in the middle. There was no grass, just weeds, and it looked like the lawn hadn't been mowed since last year.

"Home sweet home," he quipped as we walked over to him.

I couldn't help but think it would be an easy search. There was no garage, barn, or other outbuildings, and I wanted to finish up and be on my way as soon as possible.

Jimmy walked to the front door and we followed directly behind him, being sure to watch him carefully as we entered the house. Most country folk keep at least one gun in their home that is within easy reach. I always try to expect the unexpected. You can never be sure how someone might react when their life is taking a turn for the worst. Jimmy was facing a potential lawsuit from Jayson and Kyle. There would be a substantial hospital bill for their treatment, and he had to know they'd come after him for reimbursement. He was also facing a heavy fine from the Game Commission and the loss of his hunting privileges for a number of years. Desperate men have been known to resort to violent behavior in the face of despair, sometimes inflicting great harm on others as well as themselves. Although I didn't expect anything like that to happen, the possibility that it might, however remote, kept me on my toes.

The front door led to a large mudroom with a cheap linoleum tile floor. There was a stand-alone sink and a Formica countertop at the far wall. The kind you might find in a kitchen. But this one had only one purpose, and that was for cutting up game. It had been recently wiped clean, but there were a few bloodstains still on the surface. Opposite the table and sink stood a medium-sized chest freezer.

I walked over and lifted the lid. Inside I found a dozen

plastic bags full of frozen vegetables, a few beef steaks and rump roasts and two wild turkey breasts. Both were wrapped in heavy white freezer paper with the date of kill inscribed by a felt-tipped pen. The birds were shot one day apart and several days before the opening of the spring gobbler season (this was 1990). I'd done many searches over the years, and always chuckled inside when I found illegal meat in a freezer marked with a date of kill that was prior to the opener. It was amazing how often poachers helped convict themselves in this way. I suppose it was bragging rights, even if only to themselves. Perhaps the illegal meat was even more tasty when they pulled a package from the freezer with a date marking the very day that they fulfilled their illicit act.

"Like I said," declared Jimmy. "Two birds and that's all I've got."

I set the two frozen packages on the counter. "What about your kitchen?" I said. "Don't you have a freezer in there too?"

"Yeah, but there's nothing in it except stuff from the local supermarket."

"Let's take a look."

Jimmy shook his head hastily. "My wife is sleeping in the back bedroom. It's early morning. I wish you wouldn't do that."

"We'll be quiet," I said.

"Seriously. It's best not to wake her. She can be ornery when she doesn't get her sleep."

I was losing patience with Jimmy and wanted to get on my way. "Are you going to let us into your kitchen, or do I have to send my deputy out for a search warrant?"

Jimmy puffed a sigh of submission. "Just be real quiet," he insisted. Then he turned, and we followed him down a narrow hallway.

Jimmy was right about two things: there was nothing but a bunch of grocery items in his kitchen freezer, and his wife can be ornery when she doesn't get enough sleep. Just as we finished rummaging through his freezer, there came a booming voice from the back of the house.

"JIMMMMMEEEE! WHO'S OUT THERE WITH YOU?"

"Just a couple friends," he called back to her. "They're on their way out right now."

He turned to us, his face a map of despair. "Satisfied? You woke her up! Now, please go before she sees you here."

I hardly knew how to respond and wasn't about to dash out the door in order to save him from an angry wife.

"We need to look in your basement too," I said.

Jimmy lowered his voice to a whisper. "My basement!" he hissed. "Are you kidding? There's nothing down there but cobwebs!"

"We're not leaving until we take a look," I whispered in return. Then thought, why am I whispering too?

"I CAN STILL HEAR YOU OUT THERE!" came the voice once more. Louder this time, and sharper.

"Sorry dear," he called. "We're leaving right now."

Jimmy turned back to us. Desperate. "Okay! Go look. But make it fast!"

Eagar to comply this time (by the sound of the woman, I didn't want to bear the agony of her wrath), my deputy and I climbed down the cellar steps for a quick peek. Jimmy was right again, nothing but assorted odd junk and cobwebs.

"I've seen enough," I said to my deputy. "Let's get out of here. I'll file all the charges later."

We were halfway up the cellar steps, when I heard the woman's heavy footfalls on the floor above us. She was up and moving fast. And as luck would have it (the bad kind this time), we walked into the kitchen at the exact same moment as Jimmy's wife.

She was a big woman. Much bigger than Jimmy and dressed only in a terrycloth robe and slippers. Her bed hair was flat in some places while in others it looked as if a firecracker went off in her hair.

"Who are you two?" she boomed at my deputy and me.

Jimmy stood in a corner, white as a ghost.

"We're state game wardens," I said.

"What are you doing in my house?"

"Your husband gave us permission to enter your home and search for illegal game. We found two turkeys in your freezer that were killed last week. The season didn't open until today."

She whipped her head toward Jimmy. "Is that true?"

Jimmy nodded that it was.

She put her hands on her ample hips and glared at him. "You told me the season opened two weeks ago! Now look at the trouble you've brought us!"

She whipped her head back toward me; lips curled into an ugly snarl. "My wayward husband might have given you permission to come into my house, but *I* sure haven't...*AND I WANT YOU OUT OF HERE RIGHT NOW!*"

Happy to oblige, my deputy and I promptly left the premises, taking the two illegal turkey breasts on our way out the door.

G lad to be in my patrol car and away from Jimmy and his wife, I drove to the state highway and turned toward Tunkhannock Memorial Hospital to see how Jayson and Kyle were doing.

"What do you think will happen to Jimmy?" asked my deputy.

"He's going to pay a hefty fine for the two illegal turkeys, but the hunting accident will really cost him. He'll lose his license for a long time after shooting two people in mistake for game, and the Commission will tack on additional years for the turkeys in his freezer."

"I was talking about his wife," chuckled my deputy. "Not his fines. She looked like she could break him in two."

I said, "Ever hear of the old saying, happy wife, happy life? I think Jimmy is in for a lot of unhappiness in the coming days, especially when she finds out about the hunting accident."

My deputy winced. "I hope he doesn't end up in the hospital along with Jayson and young Kyle."

"By the looks of her, I think he can run a lot faster than she can," I said. "He should be fine."

My deputy chuckled at the thought of Jimmy being chased around the house by his overbearing wife, and I couldn't help but laugh along with him.

"Can we stop for a quick lunch on the way to Tyler Memorial?" he asked. "I'm starved."

"Now, you're reading my mind," I said. "The Pink Apple is just ahead. How's that sound?"

"Sounds perfect."

Author's Note

Further investigation revealed that Jimmy Jones had an extensive poaching record in neighboring Luzerne County in addition to his violations in Wyoming County. As a result, the agency review board in Harrisburg revoked his hunting and trapping privileges for ten years.

Justice is the greatest interest to man on earth. It is the ligament which holds civilized beings together.
~Daniel Webster

The Return of Butch Stryker

THE FIRST TIME I MET BUTCH STRYKER was back in 1993 when my deputy apprehended him for hunting deer without wearing fluorescent orange clothing. Because he was trespassing on private property, he fled on an ATV with my deputy in hot pursuit. What started as a minor incident resulting in a one hundred dollar fine, instead spiraled into a prolonged and aggravated confrontation resulting in utter chaos.

It all started when Deputy Gene Gaydos responded to a complaint about poaching on a large tract of land in the southern portion of my district. Darkness was setting in when he heard a rifle shot echo through the woods. It sounded close, so he pulled onto a two-track lane leading into the woods and blocked the path with his vehicle. There he waited, believing the poacher would soon come out and be intercepted.

A half hour passed, when Gaydos suddenly heard the low staccato hum of an ATV coming his way. Within seconds, the machine rounded a bend and stopped in front of his vehicle. Butch Stryker and his wife, both dressed in camouflage, stared at the uniformed deputy in surprise as they sat two-up on an ATV built for one. But as my deputy exited his vehicle to confront them, they fled through the woods on their four-wheeler.

Gaydos jumped back into his truck, dropped it into reverse, and backed onto the county road. His suspects had headed west through the trees, so he started in that direction and soon spotted their four-wheeler parked alongside a house. Thinking they had to be inside, he used his radio to call me for backup and then went to the door and knocked.

Realizing he had been discovered, Butch Stryker stepped outside. Mid-thirties and six-foot-four, he possessed the gaunt, ruddy look of a heavy drinker. His hair, the color of surface rust on metal, was pulled back into a long ponytail that fell below his shoulders.

Gaydos informed Stryker that he was trespassing on posted property and hunting without orange. Then he asked to see his hunting license.

Stryker complied, all the while grumbling about how Gaydos was harassing him and that he wanted to go back and bring the deer his wife shot out of the woods.

Gaydos wasn't about to let Stryker out of his sight and informed him that he had called me to the scene and that Stryker had to wait until I arrived before going for the deer.

Butch Stryker became highly irritated, insisting that he wanted to retrieve his deer before the coyotes found it, but Gaydos managed to hold him off until I arrived moments later.

I parked my patrol car on the street and started toward them when Stryker suddenly pivoted on his heels and ran toward his four-wheeler.

Lean and athletic, Stryker moved across his yard in the long, rapid steps of an African racing ostrich. I ran after him, ordering him to stop, but he never broke stride, and just before I reached him, he hopped on the four-wheeler and started revving the engine menacingly. For a moment, I thought he might run me down when he suddenly leaped to the ground and came charging at me.

I barely had time to react. My arms shot forward like two battering rams, palms slamming into his chest as I put my entire body into the blow. Stryker reeled backwards and tumbled clumsily over his four-wheeler, limbs flailing wildly as he crashed to the ground.

Unsnapping my handcuffs, I started after him, but Stryker jumped to his feet and came at me again, his face wild with rage. From behind, his mother and his wife came charging out of the house screaming like banshees for him to stop. They latched onto him as he was inches away from me, smothering him as they pulled and tugged at his body to draw him away.

For a moment, I was taken aback. What now? Did I have to wade through these two howling women in order to make an arrest? And then what? Risk injuring both of them over what started out as a minor game law infraction.

Then, from the corner of my eye, I saw another figure coming. It was Stryker's father, waving a stout cane over his head, threatening to bash my brains out with it. With my attention momentarily drawn toward his father, Stryker lashed out and struck me in the chin with his fist while his wife and his mother hung desperately to him. Fortunately, I saw it coming and pulled back, sustaining only a glancing blow.

Gaydos and I finally managed to get things under control, but not without the help of the Pennsylvania State Police. Stryker was taken to district court and arraigned that night. Bail was set at $30,000, which got him a free trip to jail, where he sat for several days until signing off his house, barn, and shed as security with a bondsman. In the end, he paid a $3000 fine and received eight years revocation of his hunting privileges.

Had he stopped for Deputy Gaydos when signaled, his fine would have been $100 without the likelihood of revocation. But Stryker chose to flee. And when confronted by Gaydos, he became uncooperative, his hostile behavior erupting to the point that additional officers had to be called in. As a result, Stryker's willful disregard for wildlife laws and the officers who enforce them, had cost him dearly.

But men like Butch Stryker never learn their lesson, and years later, after hearing rumors about him continuing to poach deer, I got a phone call from a man named Delmar Cribb. He was caretaker for the Chelsey property (they owned three thousand acres with a large population of whitetail deer, including many trophy bucks). Delmar claimed that he had seen Butch Stryker driving around the Chelsey property, road hunting, and asked me to take action.

Stryker lived within walking distance of Chelsey's property, which is where he fled from Deputy Gaydos on his ATV years ago. I immediately stepped up my patrols in that area, and soon ran into him again, hunting with a man named Elmer Crowe.

Crowe had just killed an illegal doe when I confronted him in the act. While questioning him about the incident, I spotted a man in camouflage clothing as he ran through the distant trees. Certain it was Stryker, I quickly ran after him, but six-foot-four Butch Stryker with his long legs and considerable head-start was way ahead of me and soon escaped on an ATV hidden in the woods.

Because I knew he was operating in the area, I went back to the Chelsey property days later to see if I could locate him. A heavy snowstorm had fallen the day before, and when I came to a bend in the road, I saw tire tracks from a vehicle that had pulled to the side and stopped. A single set of footprints zigzagged through the snow leading deep into the woods, indicating someone had been dropped off, so I parked my patrol car and started following the tracks.

Before long, I spotted Stryker in a treestand a hundred yards away, his long red hair and wiry frame unmistakable under the blazing sun. I quickly moved in, expecting him to start down the tree at any moment. But he made no effort.

When I reached the treestand, I saw it was heavily baited and felt certain I had finally caught him in the act. Dozens of bright red apples surrounded the area, and it was littered with deer tracks.

"Don't shoot!" he chuckled sarcastically. "I'm unarmed." Then he turned and began to work his way down the treestand. He was dressed in a heavy camouflage jacket that was hooded in the back and wore Carhartt field pants with steel-toe work boots and leather gloves.

After patting him down for hidden firearms (and finding none), I asked if he put the apples under the treestand.

He admitted doing it but claimed he wasn't hunting, just watching the deer. And because I didn't find a gun, he was in the clear.

I climbed up his treestand and peeked over the platform, but there were no guns or hunting equipment of any kind. From there, I started searching the surrounding area and found a .38 caliber revolver in the snow. It was an older model with a four-inch barrel, cheap to buy on the black market and perfect for shooting a deer at close range. The cylinder was empty, and I was sure the bullets were scattered in the snow, impossible to find.

Evidently, Stryker had seen me coming through the woods before I saw him, so he emptied the gun and tossed it into the snow, hurling the ammo into different directions.

In the end, I had no case. The serial number from the Taurus came back to a stolen weapon, and because Stryker was wearing gloves, there would be no fingerprints to be found anywhere.

Stryker had a way of making anything he said sound like a threat. And when I chased him off the property that day, the last words out of his mouth were cold and menacing: "I'll see you around," he said bitterly. "We'll meet again!"

And he was right.

It all started with a call from Delmar Cribb once again. Just two years earlier I had caught Cribb road hunting after he called me to report that Butch Stryker was poaching deer on the Chelsey property. Ironically, Stryker got clean away, and the only one I caught poaching was Delmar.

My deputy and I had set up a cheap plastic deer decoy in an opening along a wooded area on the Chelsey property hoping to catch Stryker shooting at it. But Delmar Cribb saw it first and shot at it right from the open window of his pickup truck.

I suspected that the only reason he called to report Stryker was because he didn't want another poacher operating on the very property he was being paid to patrol and protect from men like himself.

Although it was mid-afternoon, Delmar had been drinking and had an open can of beer in the truck when I stopped him.

His fine for shooting at the decoy was five hundred dollars, which he later paid in full. However, I gave him a break on the drinking-and-driving violation and promised not to say anything to the Chelseys as long as he drove straight home and promised to hunt lawfully in the future. Delmar probably would have been fired on the spot if the landowner knew his employee was poaching on his property. And because Delmar also lived rent free on the estate, it would have cost him dearly.

I don't know if Delmar quit poaching altogether, but I'm confident that if he didn't, he made sure not to shoot anything on the Chelsey property after that day.

"**H**e's back!" announced a frantic voice on the phone. "This is Delmar Cribb calling. Remember me?"

"Yes," I answered. Then: "Who's back?"

"Butch Stryker, that's who. And he's up to his old tricks again." There was a breathless urgency in his tone. "I tell you he's up to something out here. I've seen his pickup truck driving around real slow like. He's scouting. And he's gonna start shooting deer again. Lord knows how many this time."

"Whoa," I said. "Slow down a minute. Are you talking about the Chelsey property?"

"Yep. Sure am. And the Chelseys pay me to keep hunters off their land. So, I'm calling you to report that Butch Stryker is back. I can't catch him on my own. I'm gonna need help. And since you're The Man, I want you out here as soon as possible."

Deer season was open, but because Stryker was a convicted felon, it was unlawful for him to be in possession of any firearms, hunting or otherwise. Butch Stryker didn't worry too much about whether he was legal or not and I knew that he'd been poaching deer for the past eight years but never caught him in the act. As a result, Delmar Cribb didn't have to twist my arm to get me out to the Chelsey property, especially when I suspected that Stryker was operating there, so I assured Delmar that I would beef up my patrols in his area starting the following day.

Three thousand acres of private posted woodland is a lot of ground to cover when you're looking for signs of poaching. Especially when you have to do it from the road. The Chelsey's didn't want game wardens or any other police officers on their land, nor did they want any hunting. They looked at their property as a sanctuary for wildlife, and any form of human trespass was forbidden. I intended to respect their wishes unless I suspected poaching activity was afoot. As a state game warden, the Game Law allowed me to enter any property, posted or otherwise, in the performance of my duty. And because it was my sworn duty to uphold the law and protect the wildlife and natural resources within Pennsylvania, I intended to go wherever necessary in order to uphold my responsibilities.

Since deer season was in full swing, and I had more than a few reports of poaching in my district, I called a deputy to assist me with a search of the Chelsey estate. My plan was for both of us to cruise the township roads surrounding the property by vehicle and to initiate foot patrols if anything looked even remotely suspicious. With two men working the area, we could accomplish a sweep in half the time it would take if I were acting alone.

I wanted to catch Butch Stryker, but I also had the rest of my district to patrol for poachers. I couldn't afford to spend days on end looking for Stryker. After all, he had managed to elude me year after year for the better part of a decade. He was a formidable opponent with an extraordinary ability to avoid apprehension, and my primary responsibility was to keep vigil over all of Wyoming County, not just one small parcel of land.

It was seven o'clock in the morning as my deputy and I began our patrol of the Chelsey estate. We went in opposite directions, one heading east, the other west, but after hours of patrol we didn't find anything that indicated there was any hunting in the area, let alone poaching activity.

We were about to break for a quick lunch with plans to patrol the remainder of my district when the Game Commission regional office contacted me by radio.

"Some guy wants you to call him," said the dispatcher. "Won't give his name. Says it's about hunting over bait."

"Is the violation in progress?"

"He says it is. I have a phone number if you want it."

"Affirmative," I replied, reaching for a notepad and pen.

After copying down the number my dispatcher provided, I drove to a nearby gas station with a phone booth outside to make the call. I parked my patrol car out of the way, walked over to the booth and punched in the phone number I was given. On the third ring, I heard a metallic *click* indicating someone had picked up.

"Hello?" I said.

"Wasserman?" asked a voice on the other end. Even though it had been years since my last contact with Stryker, I recognized the voice immediately. It was the way he said my name…the threatening tone in his voice.

"That's right," I said.

"I hear you've been looking for me."

Surprised he'd been alerted, I played dumb. It would only make him all the more difficult to catch if he knew I was after him. "I'm too busy to spend time looking for you, Stryker," I said. "What do you want?"

"I know who contacted you: it was Delmar Cribb. He sicked you on me because he don't want nobody shooting deer on Chelsey's land but himself." He paused for a moment, then: "Look, Wasserman, I admit I hunt on Chelsey's property, so does Cribb and a bunch of others, but I only kill to feed my family."

I said, "If you can't provide for your family, you can always apply for government assistance."

"Don't worry," scoffed Stryker. "I get my monthly check from Uncle Sam. But it ain't enough. So, yeah, I take a few more deer than I'm supposed to, but Chelsey's land is overrun with them. I'm actually doing good by keeping the herd in check."

"That's your opinion, not mine," I said.

"I don't expect you to agree with me, and I don't care. You're wasting your time looking for me; you should be going after Roscoe Stoner. He's been killing deer and turkeys around here for years. He baits them in and shoots all year long."

"Why are you telling me this?" I asked.

Stryker surprised me with his answer. "I owe you one," he said. "You helped my old man get his hunting license back a few years ago. It changed his life. Besides, I don't like Stoner and I'm sick of him bragging about how he's the Great White Hunter and all that kind of trash talk. Anybody can shoot a deer over bait. That don't take no skill."

You should know, I thought. Then said: "I'm listening."

"Stoner has fifty acres adjoining Chelsey's land. Just follow Hayfield Road along Chelsey's property until you come to Creek Road. Turn left and go about a quarter mile and you'll come to a house on your left. That's Stoner's place. Go another two hundred yards; you'll come to a bridge. Park on the other side of the bridge and you'll see where he drives his truck back into the woods. Follow the tracks and you'll find the bait. Lots of it. He's got three treestands back there too."

Suddenly I heard the droning hum of a line gone dead. Stryker had hung up without another word.

Because my patrol car was equipped with emergency lights and marked with emblems identifying it as a Game Commission vehicle, my deputy and I drove to the bridge on Creek Road in his unmarked pickup truck. The bridge had been built long ago and was much larger than it needed to be for the small stream to pass below. Fortunately for us, once we crossed and pulled to the berm, the road dropped off, which kept my deputy's truck out of view from Stoner's house.

Just as Stryker had said, there were tire tracks leading through a weedy field into the woods. The area was posted against trespassing, which was no surprise. Suspecting Stryker's tip was valid, my deputy and I slid out of his vehicle

149

and began following the tire tracks on foot as they wound their way back into the woods.

Because it was early afternoon, and the risk of being observed by other motorists was high, we moved fast, hoping to find the baited area and get out before being detected.

Deputy points to apples in weeds between tire tracks.

As we followed the tracks, we found where a few apples had fallen from the truck in several spots, so we knew we were on to something positive. After traveling three hundred yards into the woods, we came to an area baited with fresh apples, salt blocks, and a grain feeder loaded with cracked corn. The grain feeder had been placed months ago judging by the way the ground surrounding it had been trampled with deer tracks.

We collected a handful of corn kernels, a few apples, and a walnut-sized piece of salt block for evidence, then we photographed the entire area and quickly left before anyone came by. Our plan was to return the following morning in hopes of catching the poachers on stand while hunting over the bait.

Mineral block on Stoner's property. Ball cap illustrates size of block.

Apples and salt block. Ballpoint pen illustrates size of block.

Ground trampled smooth under grain feeder behind Stoner residence.

Early the following morning, as the sky was starting to peak above the horizon, I crossed over the bridge on Creek Road and parked my patrol car along the road shoulder. My deputy had to report to his regular job today (all Game Commission deputies are part time volunteers), and I was alone. But the fact that I might have to confront three armed hunters by myself didn't worry me. My primary concern was that I might be shot in mistake for a deer as I approached the baited area. The woods were thick here, so I waited until the morning brightened before exiting my vehicle. I wore an orange vest and ballcap, both accented with an embroidered badge on the front as I moved quietly through the woods, pausing every few yards to scan the distant trees for any sign that a hunter might be present. As I approached within a hundred yards of the baited area, I could see someone in one of the treestands. He was dressed in camouflage, his back turned to me. The other two treestands slowly came into view as I crept closer through the woods. Both were also occupied by camouflaged hunters.

And they were watching me.

"State game warden!" I called out. *"Keep your rifles pointed in the air!"*

I moved faster now, observing the men closely as I marched ahead. When I reached the baited turf directly under them, I ordered all three to unload their firearms and come down from their treestands with the action open.

When they climbed down, I had each man lean his rifle against the base of his tree and stay there.

"Which one of you is Roscoe Stoner?" I said to them.

"That would be me," replied one. He was barrel-chested with a heavy beard and piercing blue eyes. "You better have a search warrant," he warned. "My land is posted, and you got no right to be here without one."

"I have every right to be here," I said. "Now I want everyone to turn around so I can see your hunting licenses."

Stoner's two companions turned their backs to me. Both had a cased hunting license pinned to their backs. Stoner refused to budge.

"This is private property," he said, and I want you off my land!"

"All three of you are under arrest right now," I told him. "And the more you resist, the higher your fines will be, so I suggest you cooperate."

"Come on, Roscoe," insisted one of the men. "The man is a police officer; you need to back off."

Roscoe Stoner grumbled some choice words under his breath and turned his back to me. Relieved that I didn't have to deal with any more hostility, I took hunting licenses from each man and pocketed them, then I gathered their rifles and escorted them back to my patrol car where I wrote down the serial numbers from each firearm along with the other information I needed for my citations.

In the end, each man was charged with attempting to unlawfully kill a deer through the use of bait and fined eight hundred dollars. I didn't have sufficient probable cause to secure a search warrant for Stoner's house, nor did I have any evidence that a deer had been killed recently or the fines might have been much higher. However, in addition to their fines, they each had their hunting licenses revoked for one year. I also posted Stoner's property with official Game Commission signs stating that it was a baited area and closed to hunting for the remainder of the season. But the real payoff for me was that Stoner understood that I was aware of his practice of hunting over bait, and that he would never know when I might return in the future, so his days of poaching deer and other wildlife on his land were over.

Twenty-four Hours Later

"Dallas to five-three-eight..."

I lifted my microphone from its catch on the dashboard of my patrol car and keyed it. "Five-three-eight. Go ahead."

"It's the same guy who called two days ago," replied a dispatcher, his voice clearly agitated. "The one who called about hunting over bait. Still won't give his name. He wants you to call him."

"Ten-four," I replied.

I drove to a nearby phonebooth and dialed Stryker's number. Once again, he picked up on the third ring.

"I see you got him," he said. "And his two dopey friends."

"That's right."

"We're done now," he declared. His voice was flat and resolute. "We're even for you helping my old man."

"Understood."

"I'm gonna keep doing what I do, and you're gonna keep looking for me aren't you?"

"Yup."

"I'll be looking for you too, Wasserman," he warned. "We'll see how that turns out, won't we?"

"We sure will."

Stryker snickered under his breath. "You game wardens have a dangerous job."

"Is that right?"

"Yeah, because you never know when somebody might take a shot at you...in mistake for a deer, I mean. Ever think about that?"

"Is that a threat?"

"Just sayin' that's all."

Suddenly the line went dead, and an icy chill ran down the center of my spine. There was no doubt in my mind that Butch Stryker was capable of carrying out his threat. He was a convicted felon with a violent criminal record, which meant he could go back to prison if I caught him in possession of a firearm.

I knew I'd have to be careful the next time I confronted Butch Stryker. And that time did come. Years later. But that's a story for another day.

William Wasserman, a third-degree black belt in the Korean martial art of *Tang Soo Do* and a former national bodybuilding champion, has written twelve books about his life as a state game warden. He received numerous awards for his work in wildlife conservation, including the United Bowhunters of Pennsylvania Game Protector of the Year Award, Pennsylvania Game Commission Northeast Region Outstanding Wildlife Conservation Officer, National Society Daughters of the American Revolution Conservation Medal, and the Pennsylvania Trappers Association Presidential Award. Wasserman has been published in several national magazines including *Black Belt, Pennsylvania Game News, Fur-Fish-Game, South Carolina Wildlife, International Game Warden,* and *The Alberta Game Warden.* Wasserman retired from the Pennsylvania Game Commission after thirty-two years of dedicated service and lives in South Carolina with his wife, Maryann.

POACHER HUNTER

WILLIAM WASSERMAN

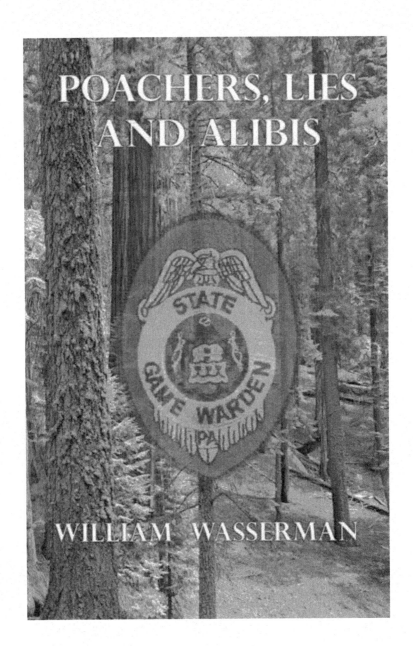

POACHERS, LIES AND ALIBIS

WILLIAM WASSERMAN